RAW ART

THE ILLUSTRATED LIVES & IDEAS OF
ROBERT ANTON WILSON

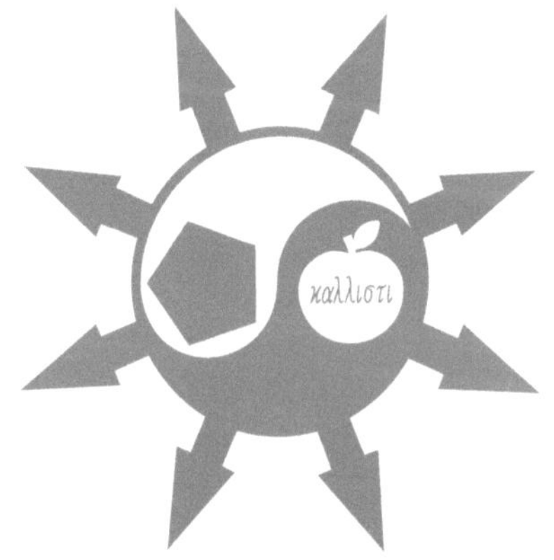

BY BOBBY CAMPBELL

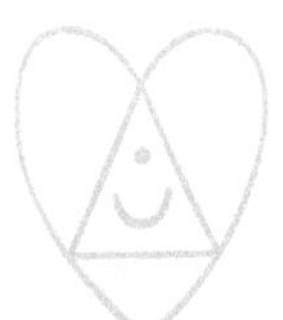

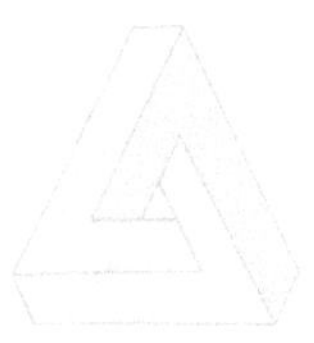

HILARITAS PRESS

RAW ART

THE ILLUSTRATED LIVES & IDEAS OF ROBERT ANTON WILSON

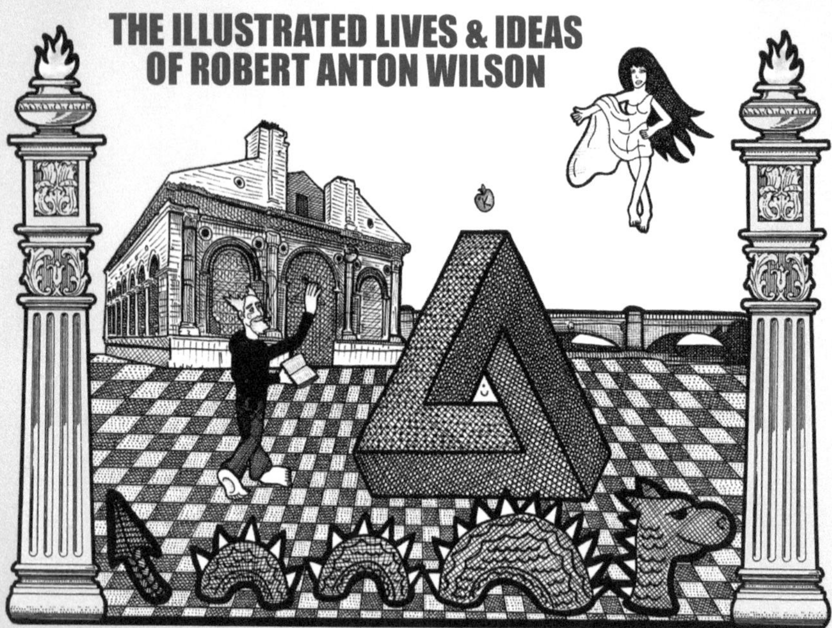

BY BOBBY CAMPBELL @RGC777
WEIRDOVERSE.COM

First Edition 2017 • eBook Version 1.0 - 2017, Hilaritas Press

Cover and eBook design by Bobby Campbell • ISBN-13: 978-0-9987134-1-0

⊚ HILARITAS PRESS

P.O. BOX 1153 GRAND JUNCTION, COLORADO 81502
WWW.HILARITASPRESS.COM

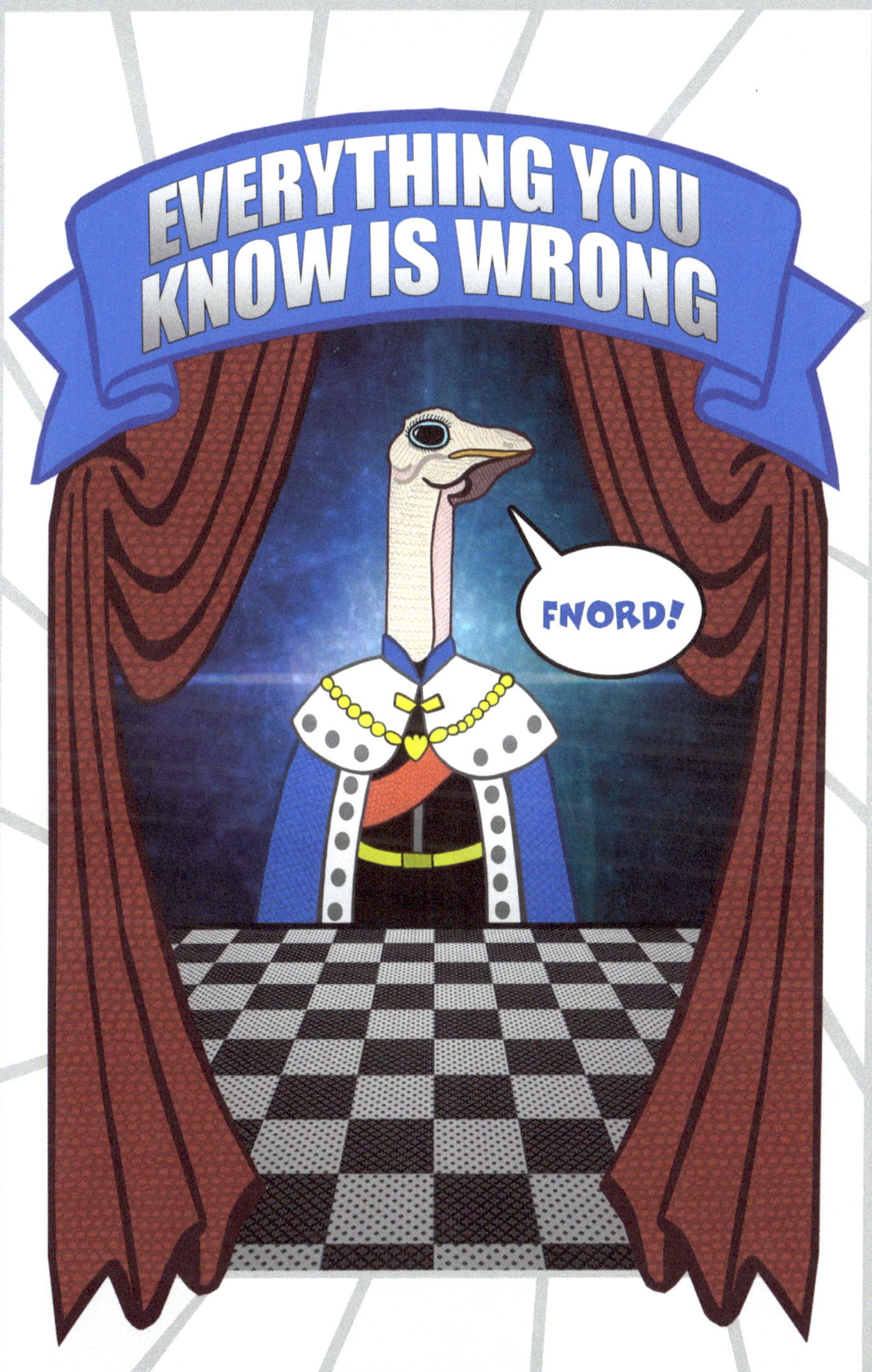

EVERYTHING YOU KNOW IS WRONG
FNORD!

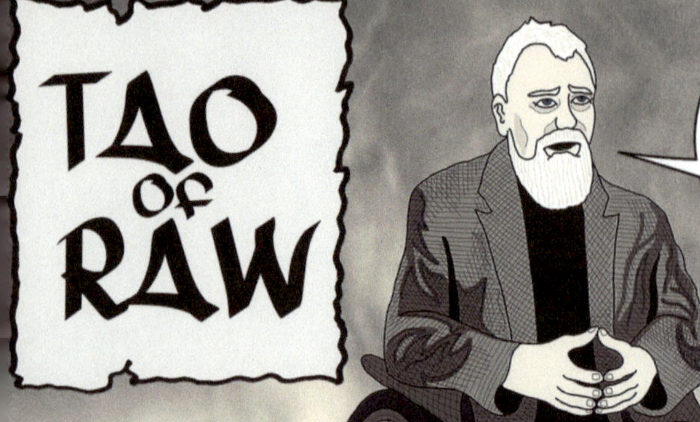

TAO OF RAW
AFTER YEARS OF VEHEMENT AND PASSIONATE STUDY OF THE IDEOGRAMS OF THE TAO TE CHING, I THINK I HAVE SUMMARIZED IT ALL INTO A COUPLE OF WORDS...

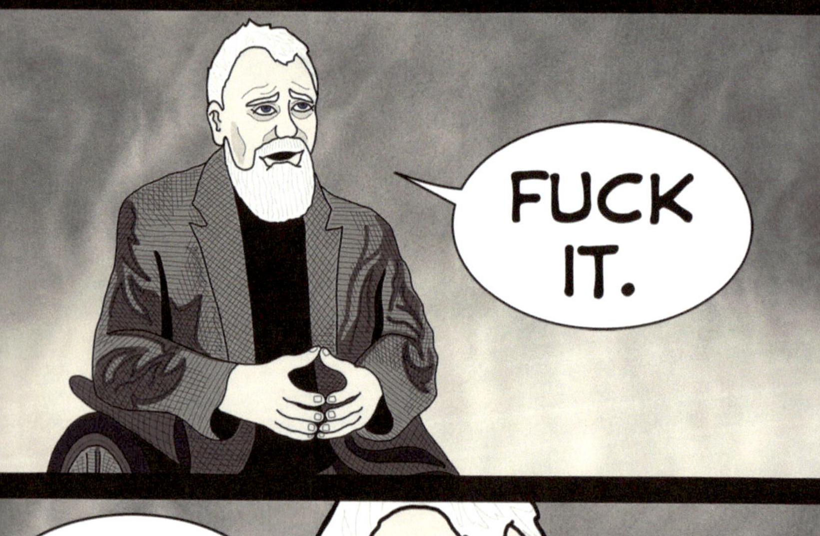

FUCK IT.

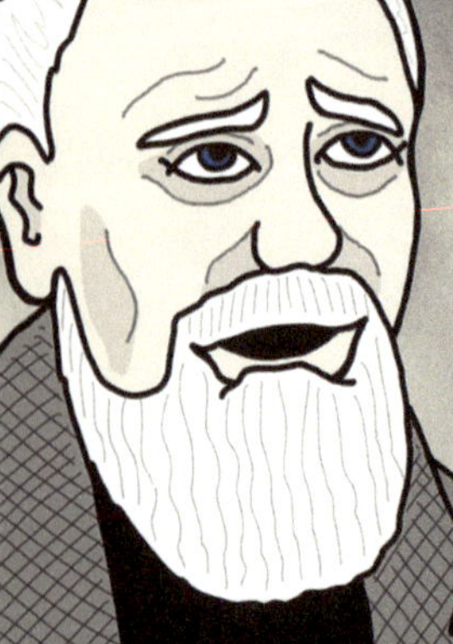

AND IF YOU CAN'T FUCK IT, IGNORE IT.
IT'LL GO AWAY.

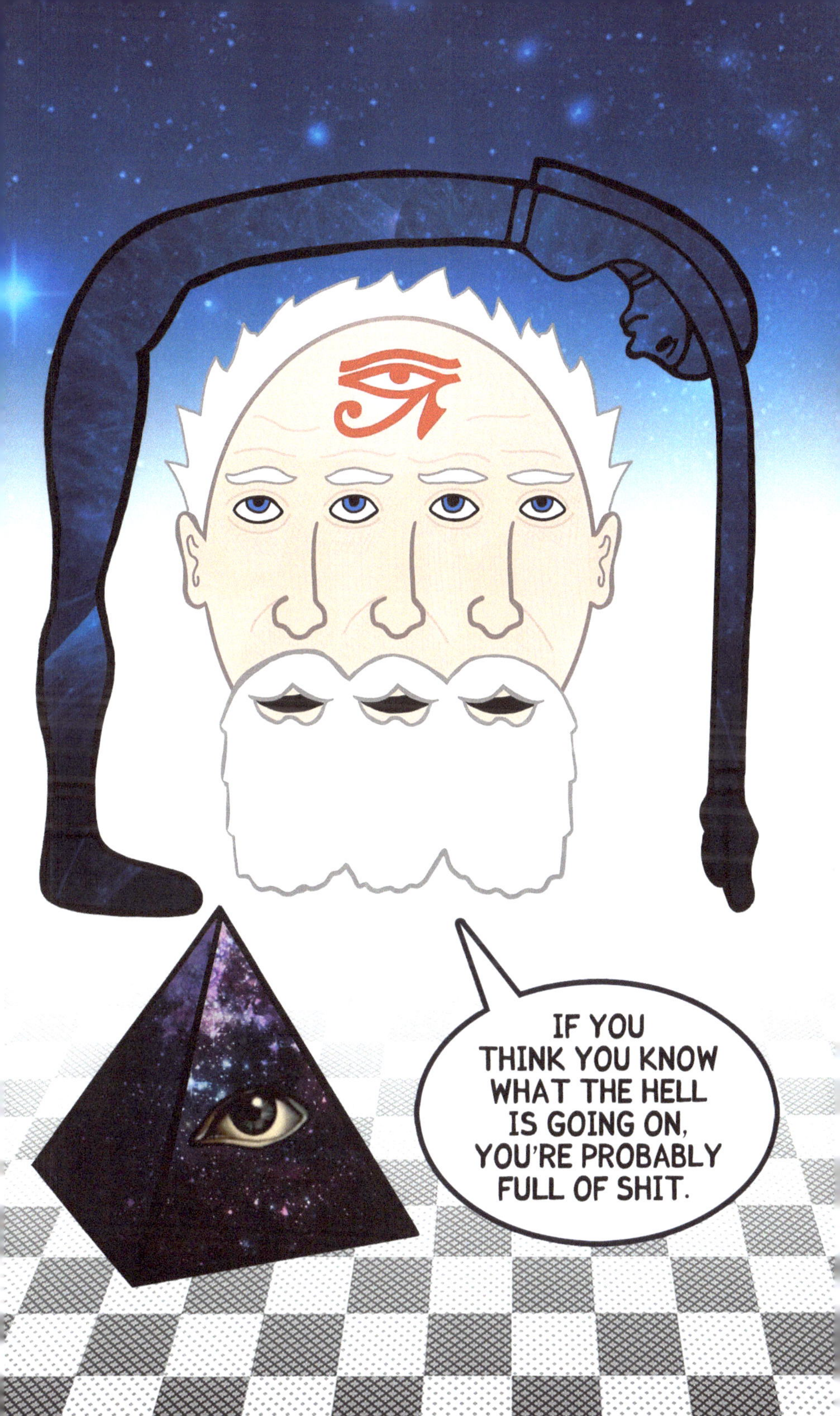

IF YOU THINK YOU KNOW WHAT THE HELL IS GOING ON, YOU'RE PROBABLY FULL OF SHIT.

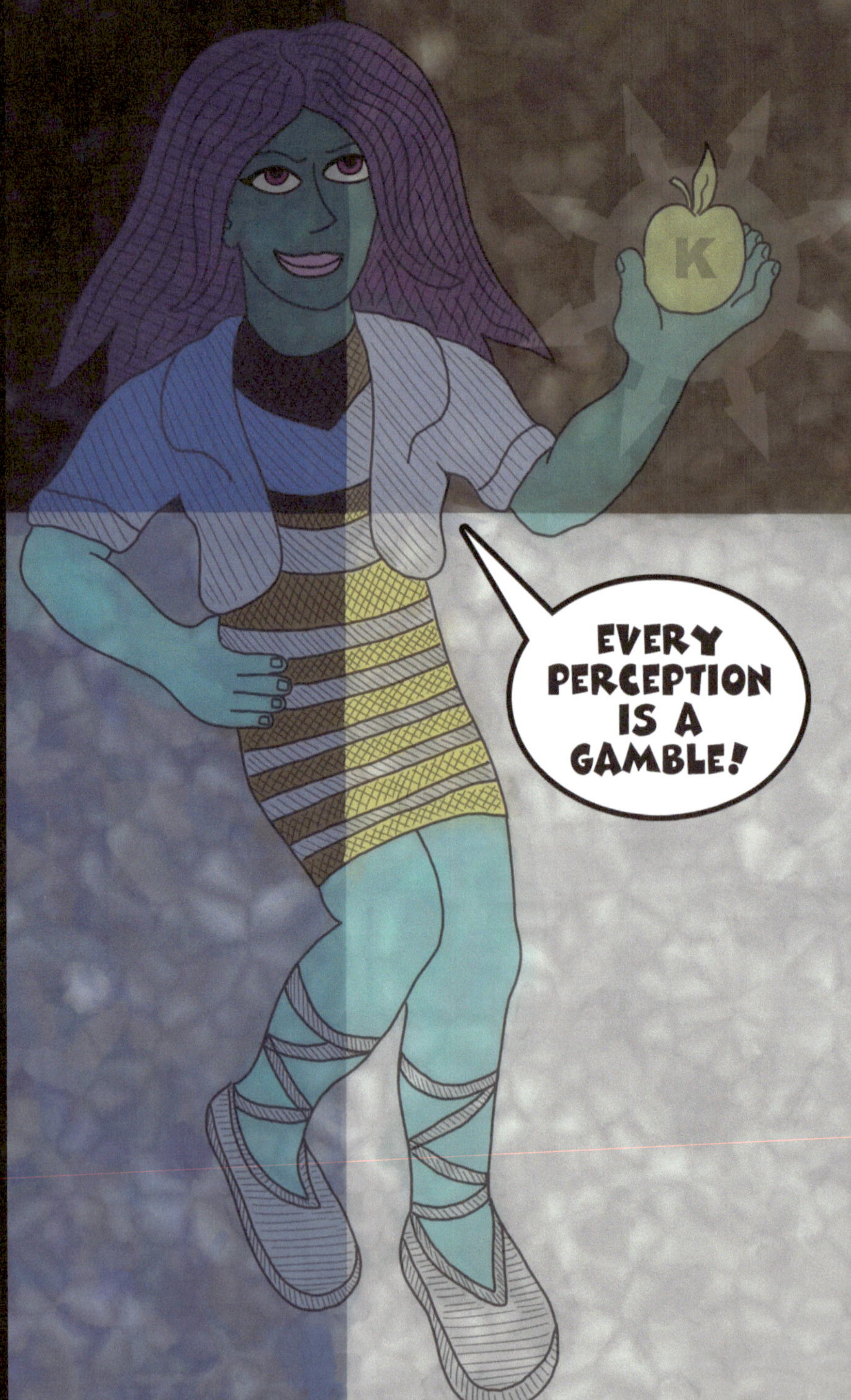
K
EVERY PERCEPTION IS A GAMBLE!

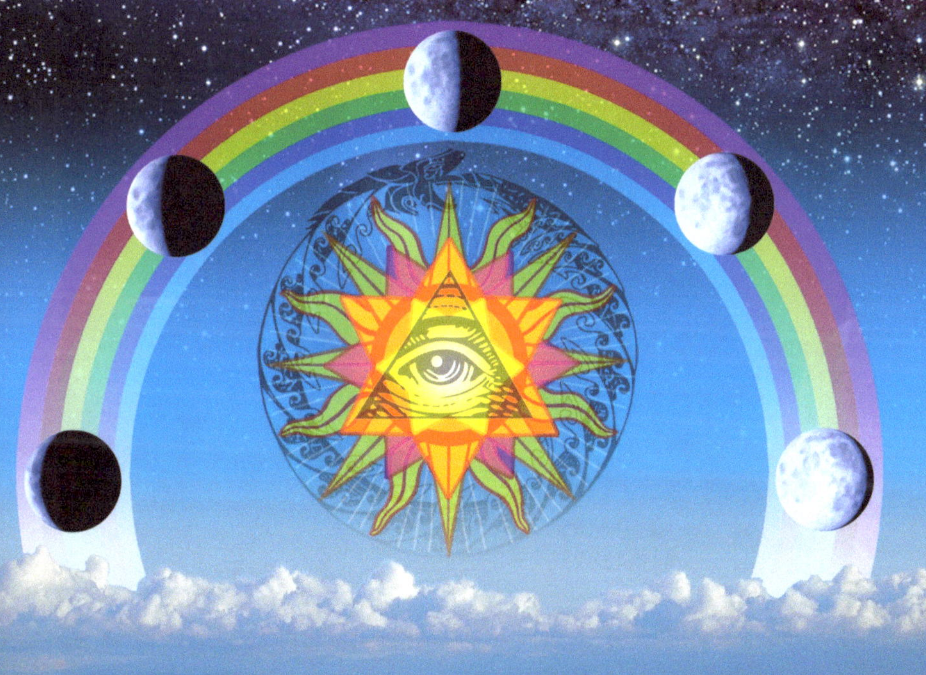
IN ADDITION TO
A YES AND NO
THE UNIVERSE
CONTAINS A MAYBE

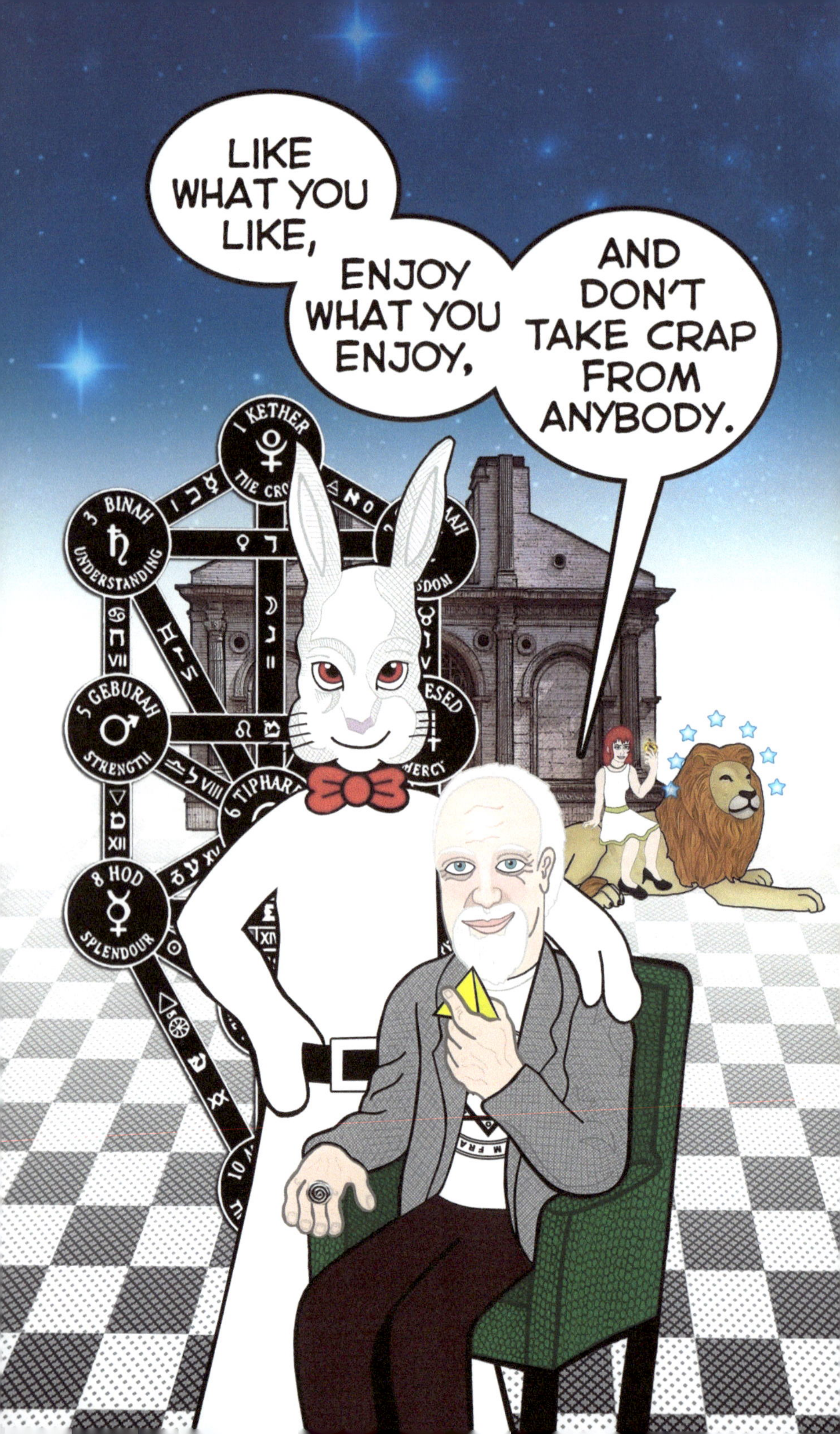

LIKE WHAT YOU LIKE,
ENJOY WHAT YOU ENJOY,
AND DON'T TAKE CRAP FROM ANYBODY.

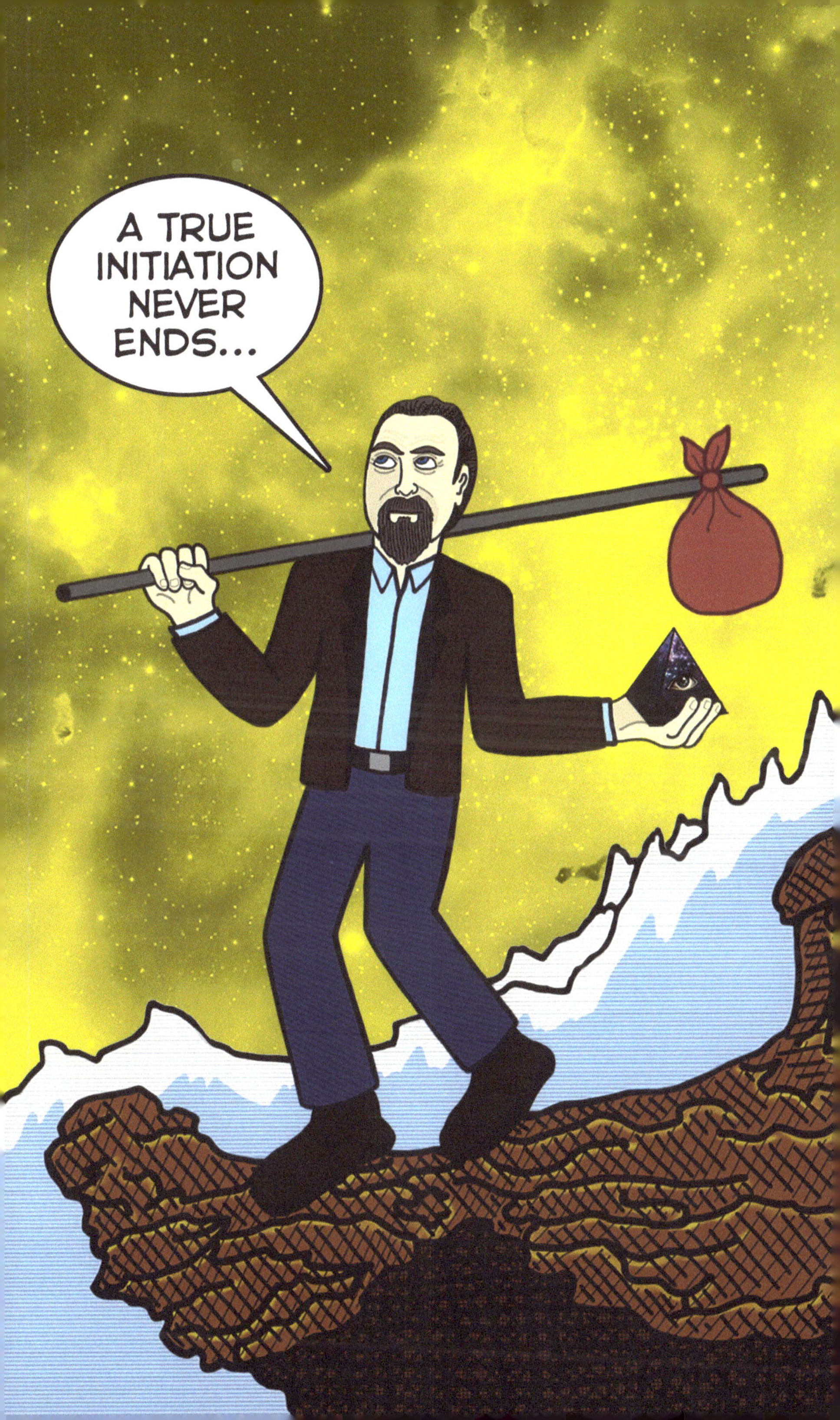

A TRUE
INITIATION
NEVER
ENDS...

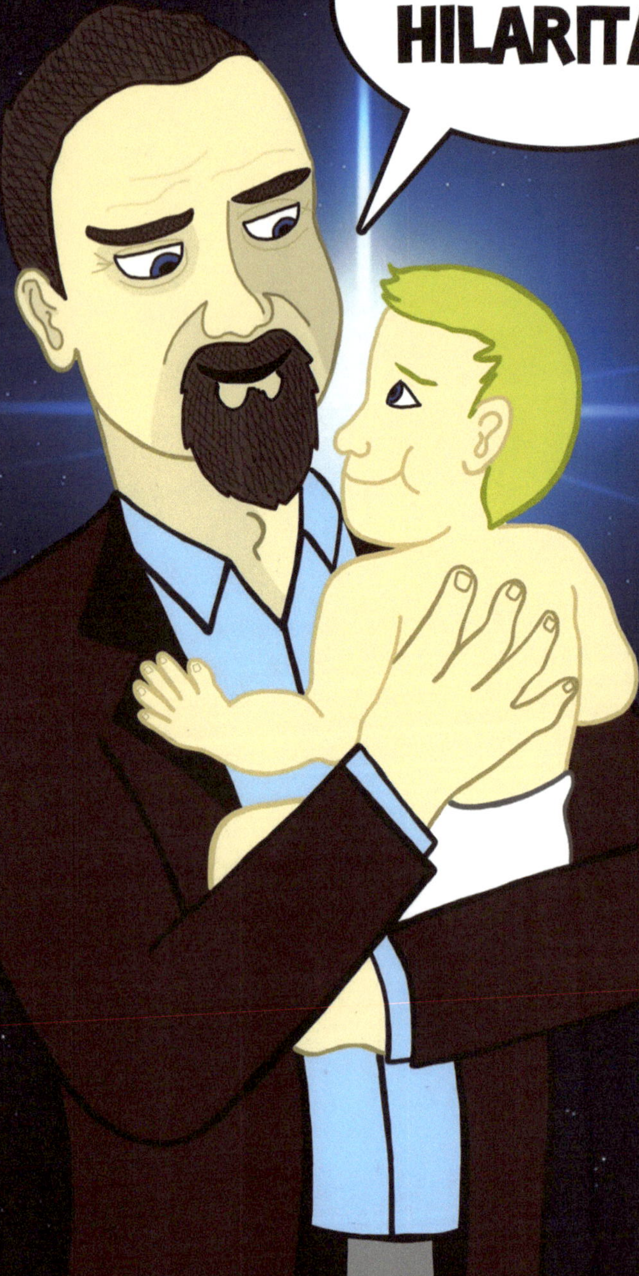

AMOR ET HILARITAS!

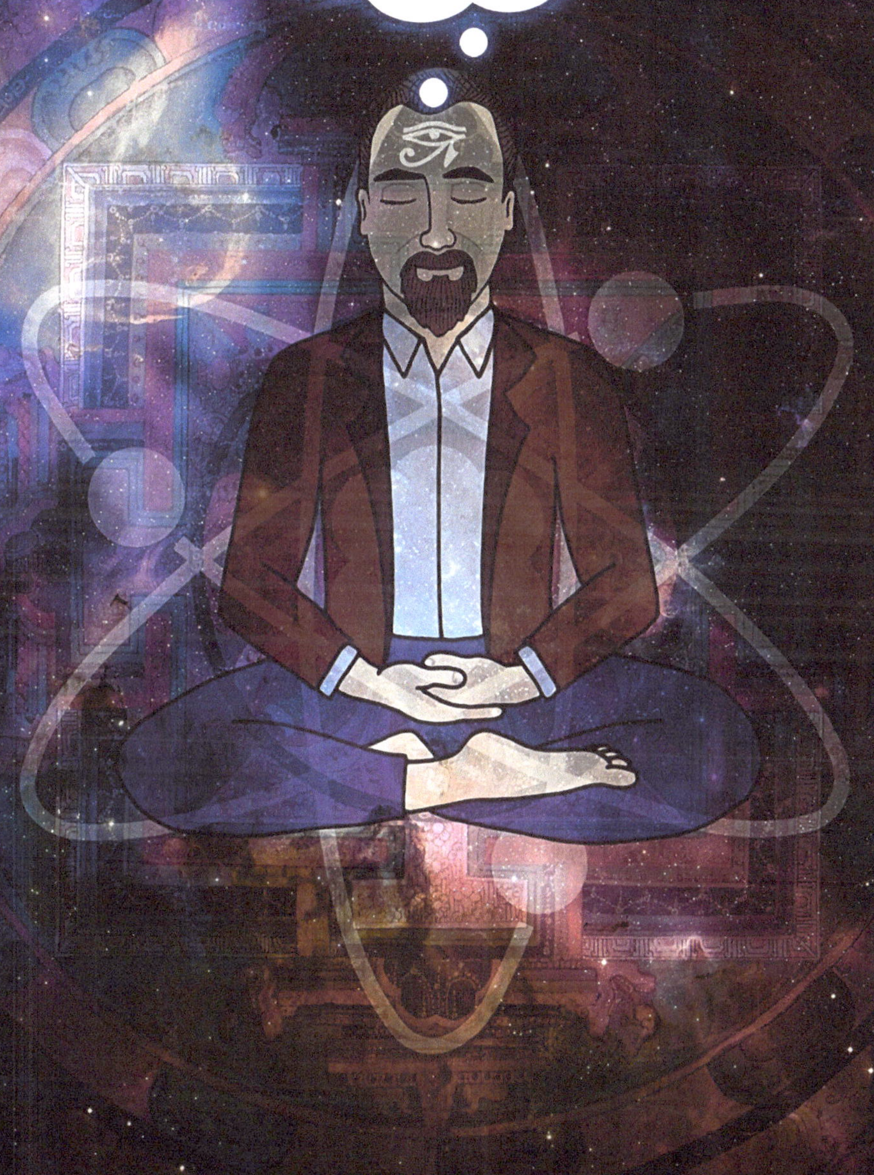
NAMU AMIDA BUTSU

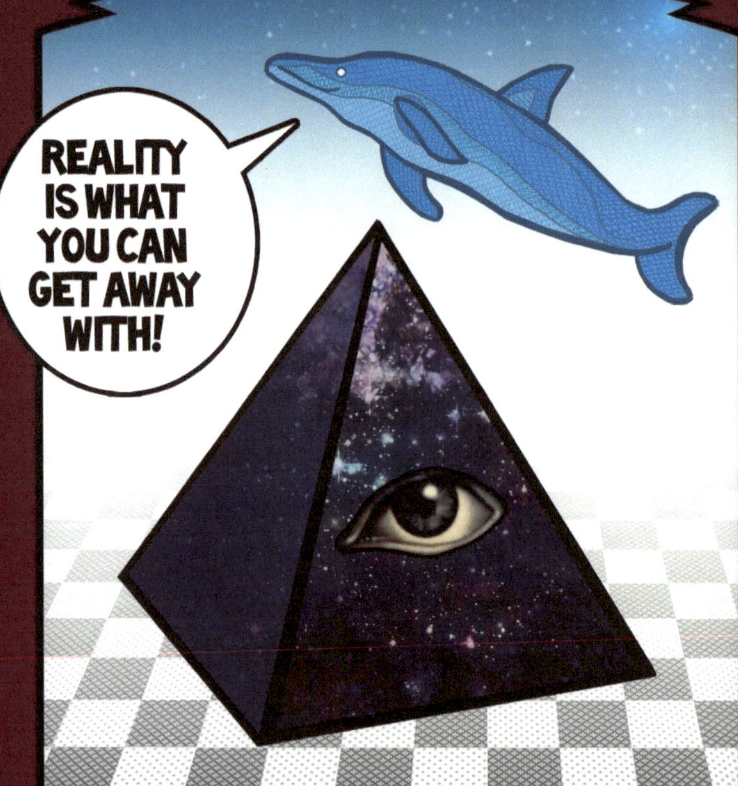

I DREAM OF
ILLUMINATUS!
IN THE WEIRDOVERSE NEXT DOOR
REALITY IS WHAT YOU CAN GET AWAY WITH!

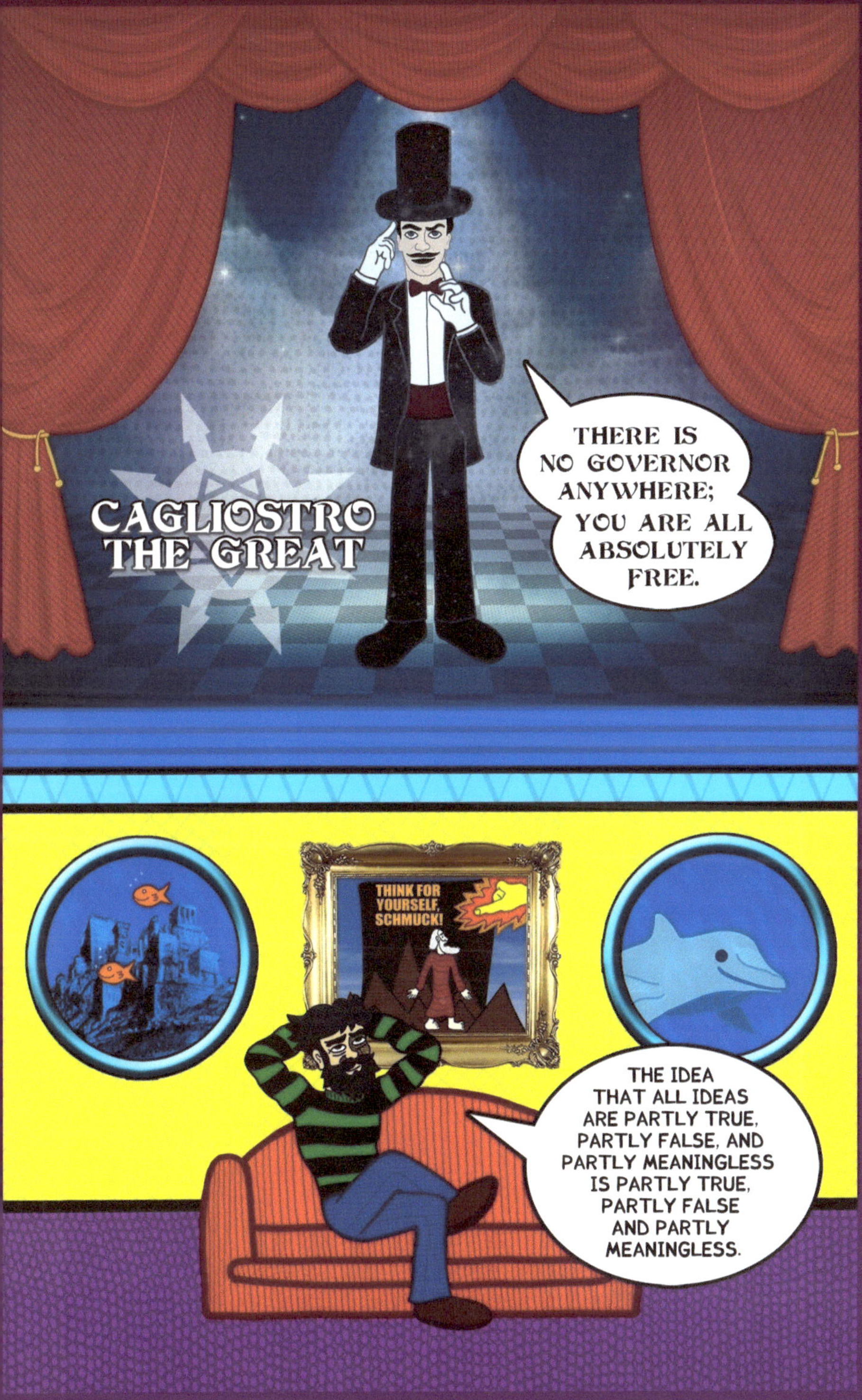

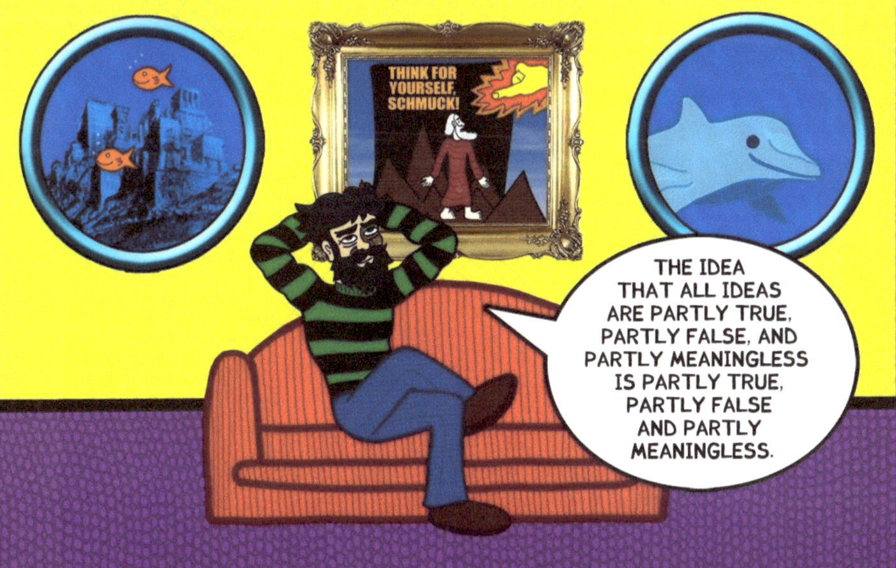

CAGLIOSTRO THE GREAT
THERE IS NO GOVERNOR ANYWHERE; YOU ARE ALL ABSOLUTELY FREE.
THINK FOR YOURSELF, SCHMUCK!
THE IDEA THAT ALL IDEAS ARE PARTLY TRUE, PARTLY FALSE, AND PARTLY MEANINGLESS IS PARTLY TRUE, PARTLY FALSE AND PARTLY MEANINGLESS.

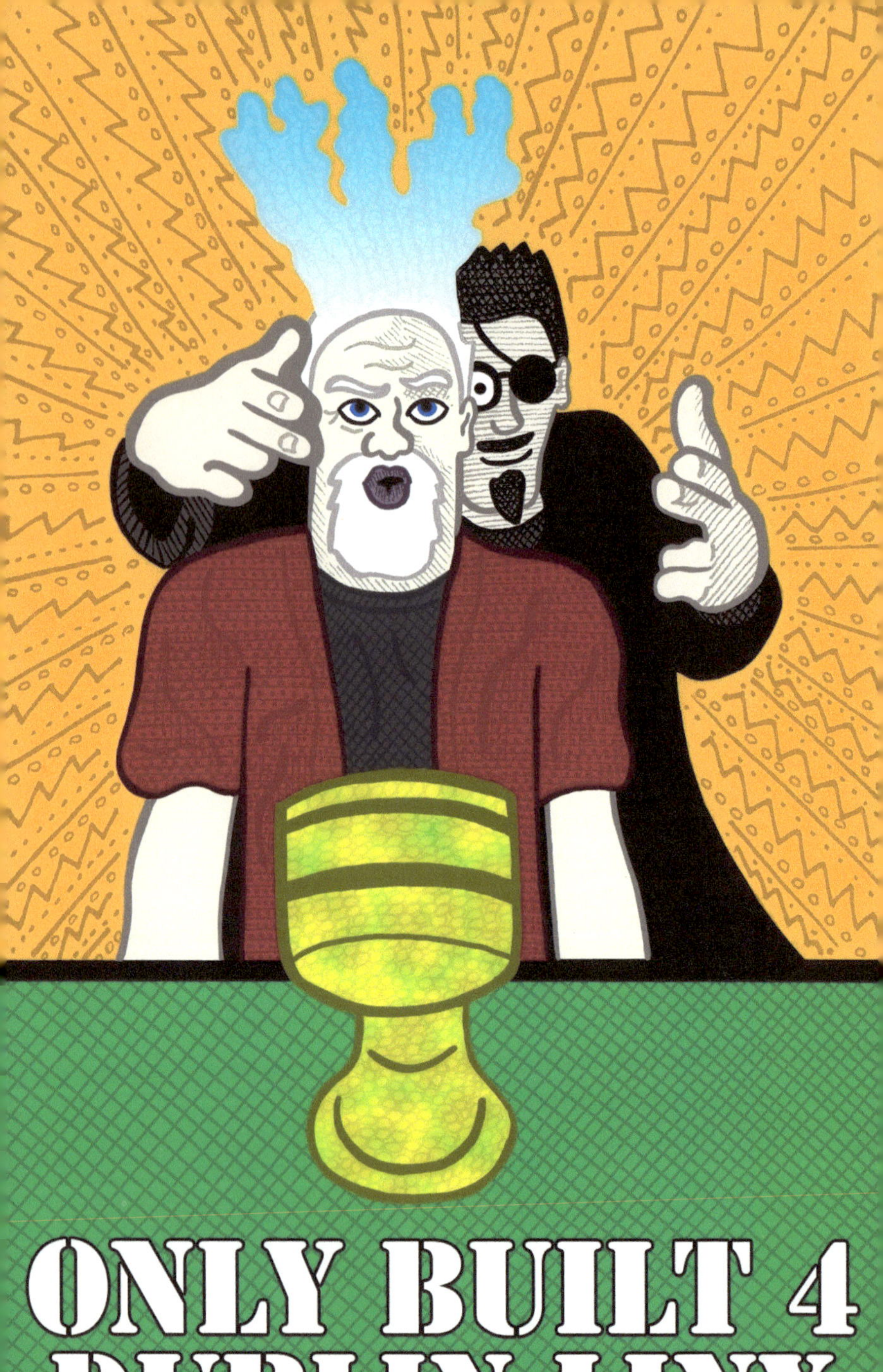

ONLY BUILT 4
DUBLIN LINX

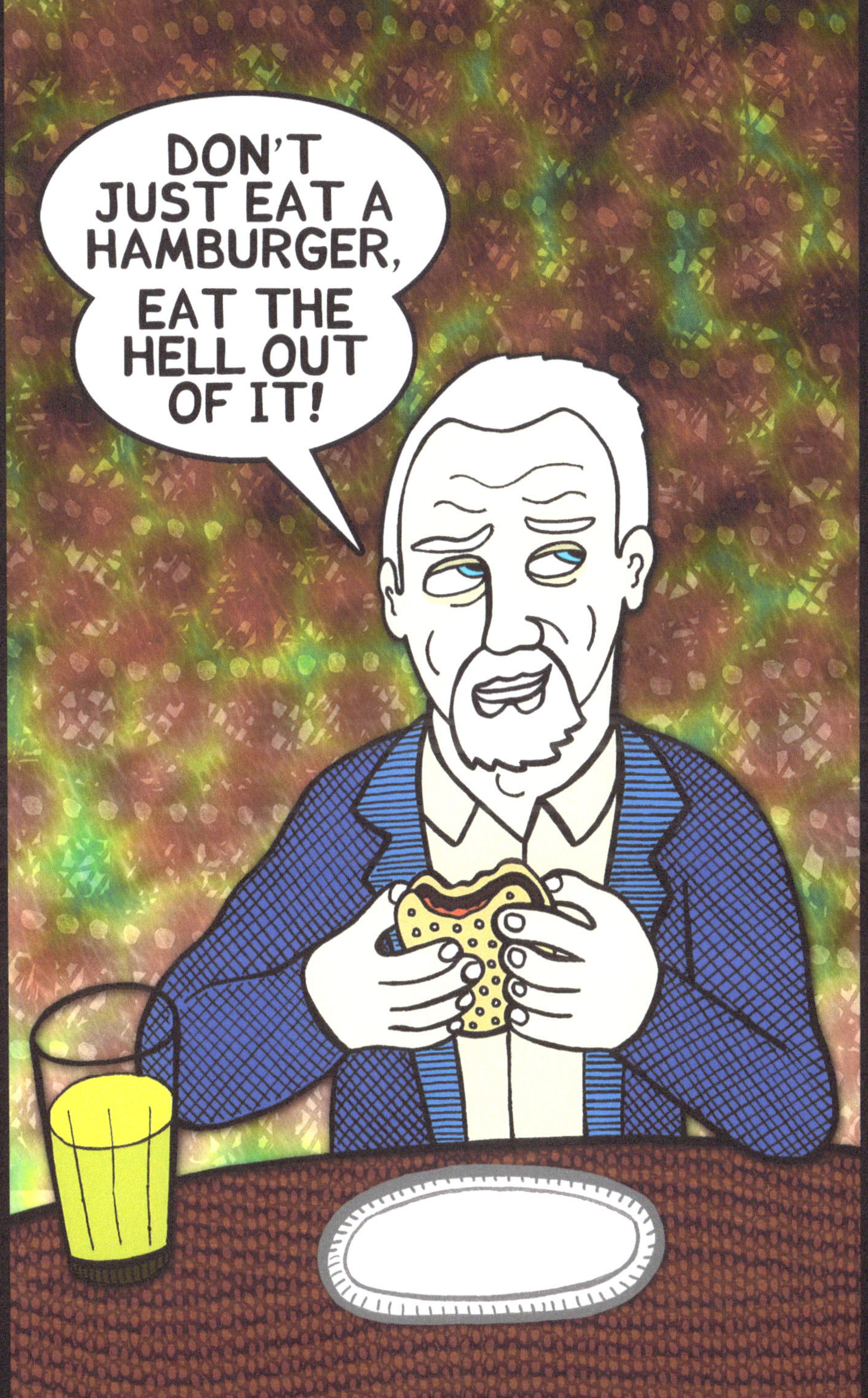

DON'T
JUST EAT A
HAMBURGER,
EAT THE
HELL OUT
OF IT!

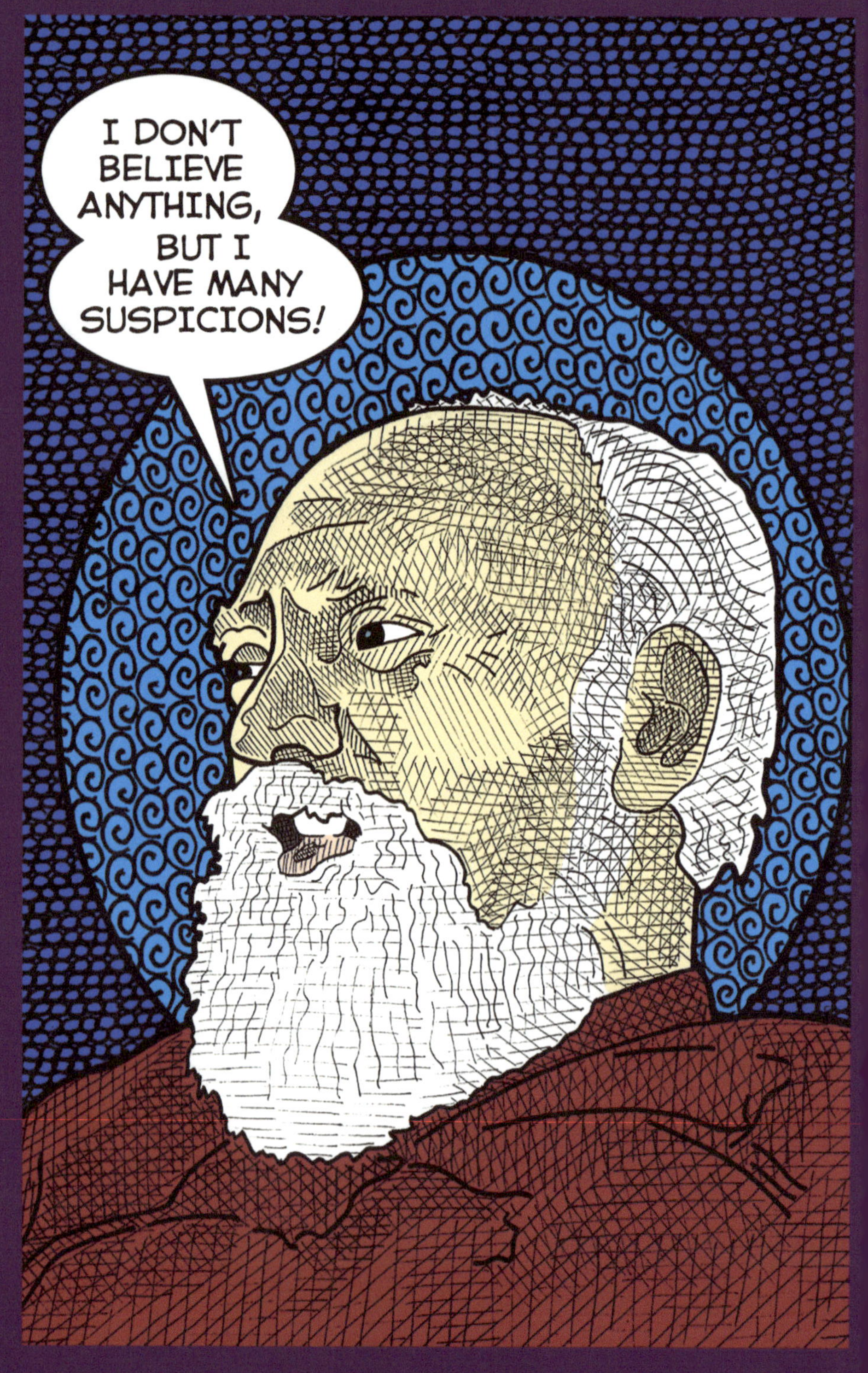

I DON'T BELIEVE ANYTHING, BUT I HAVE MANY SUSPICIONS!

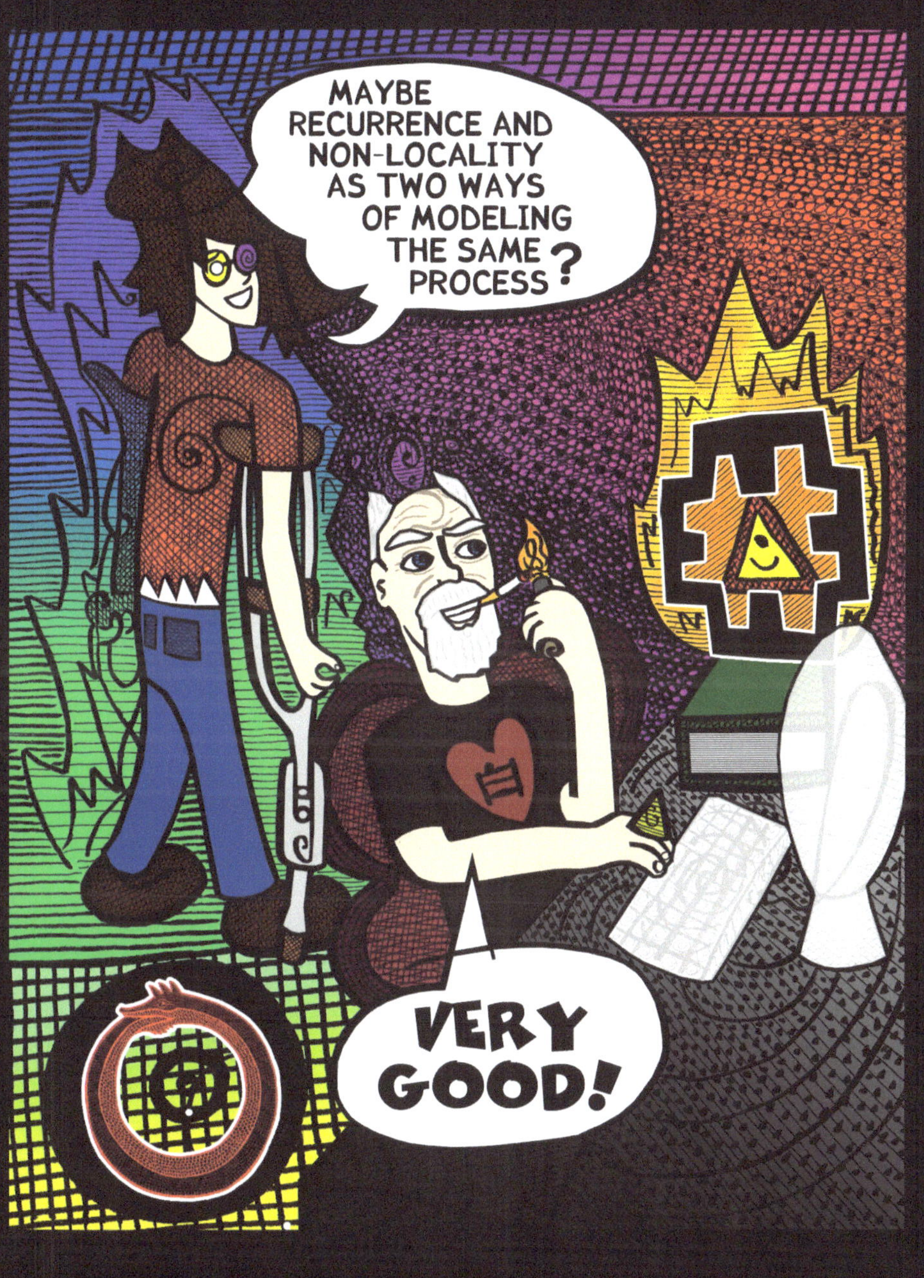

MAYBE RECURRENCE AND NON-LOCALITY AS TWO WAYS OF MODELING THE SAME PROCESS?
VERY GOOD!

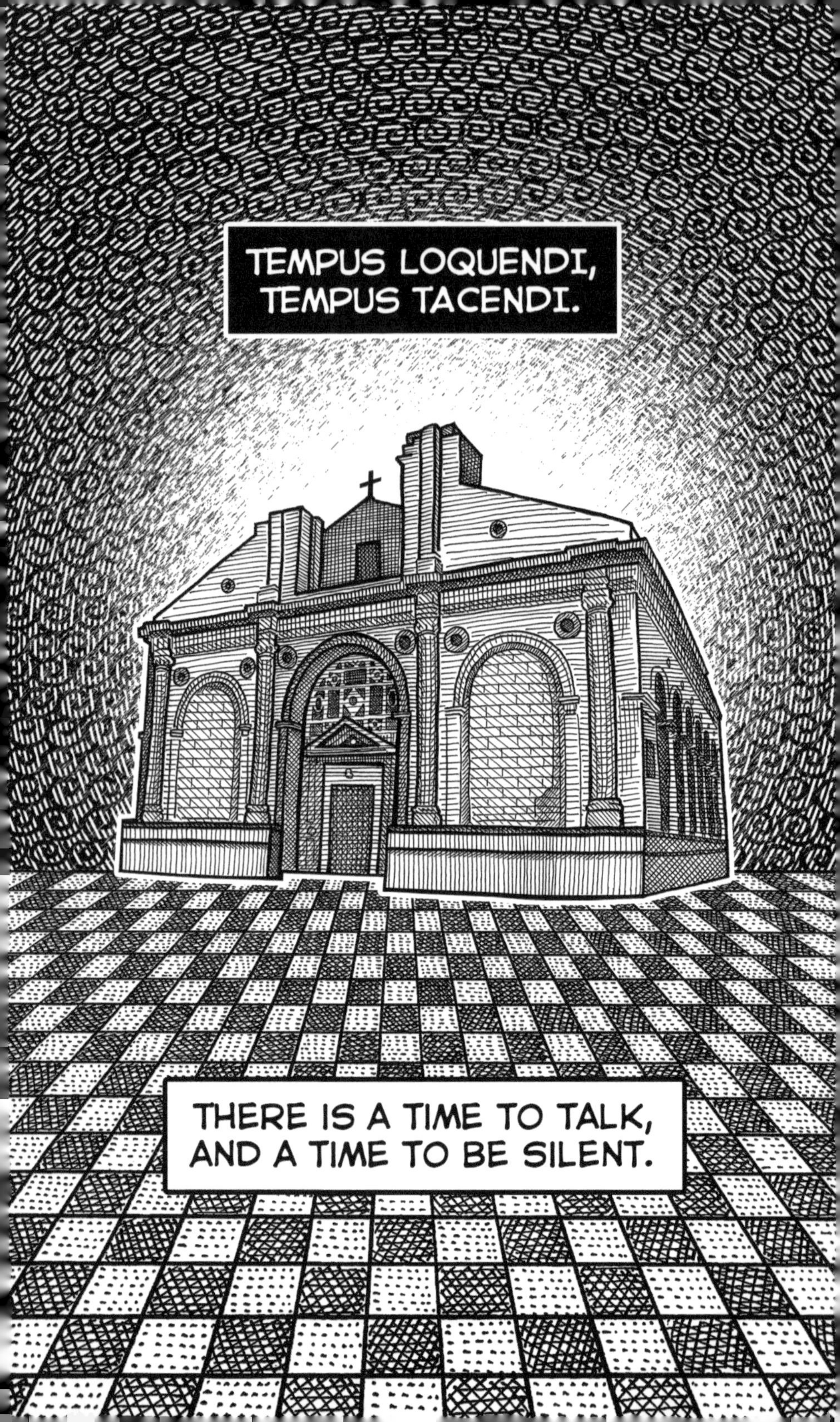

TEMPUS LOQUENDI, TEMPUS TACENDI.
THERE IS A TIME TO TALK, AND A TIME TO BE SILENT.

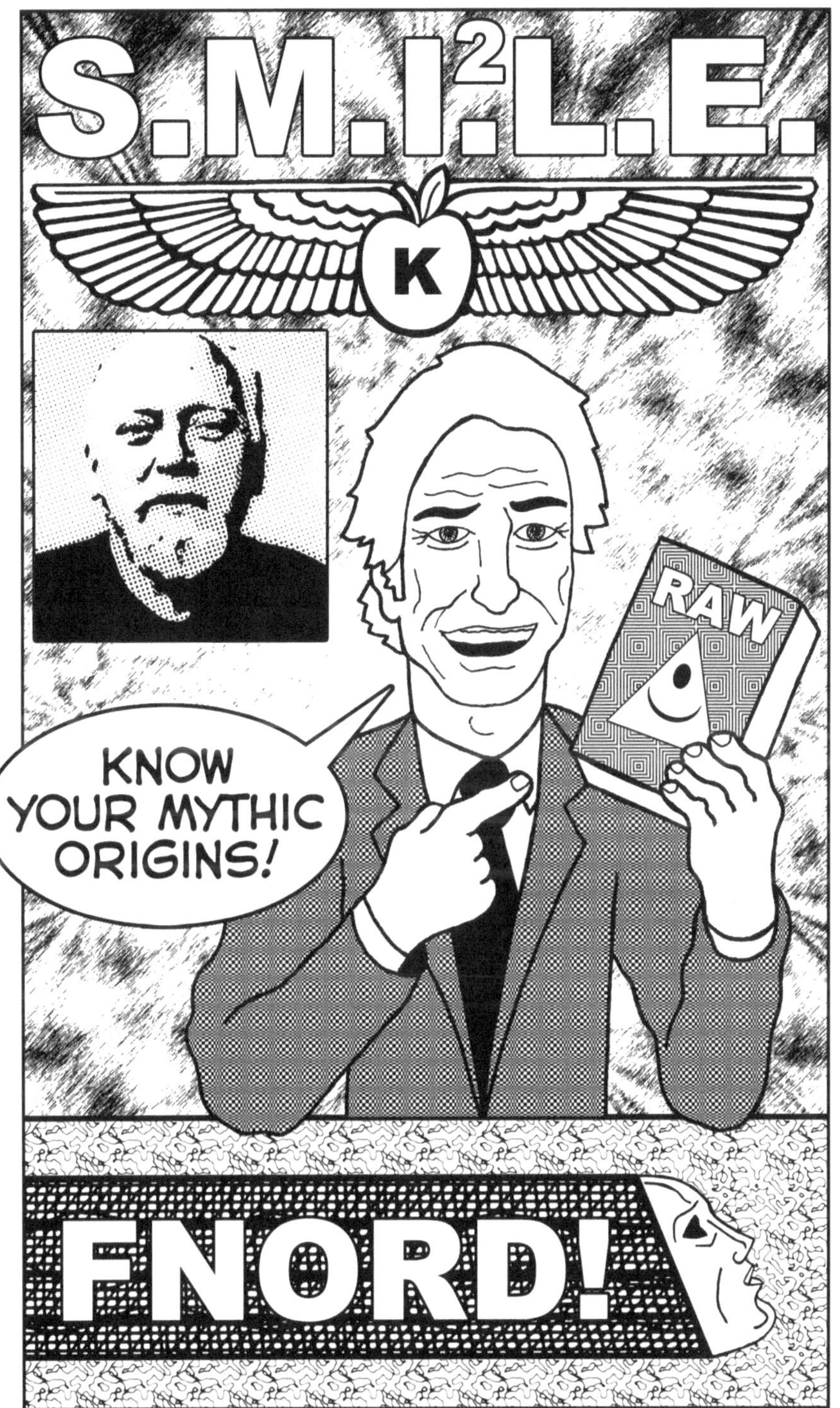

S.M.I²L.E.
K
KNOW YOUR MYTHIC ORIGINS!
RAW
F.NO²RD!

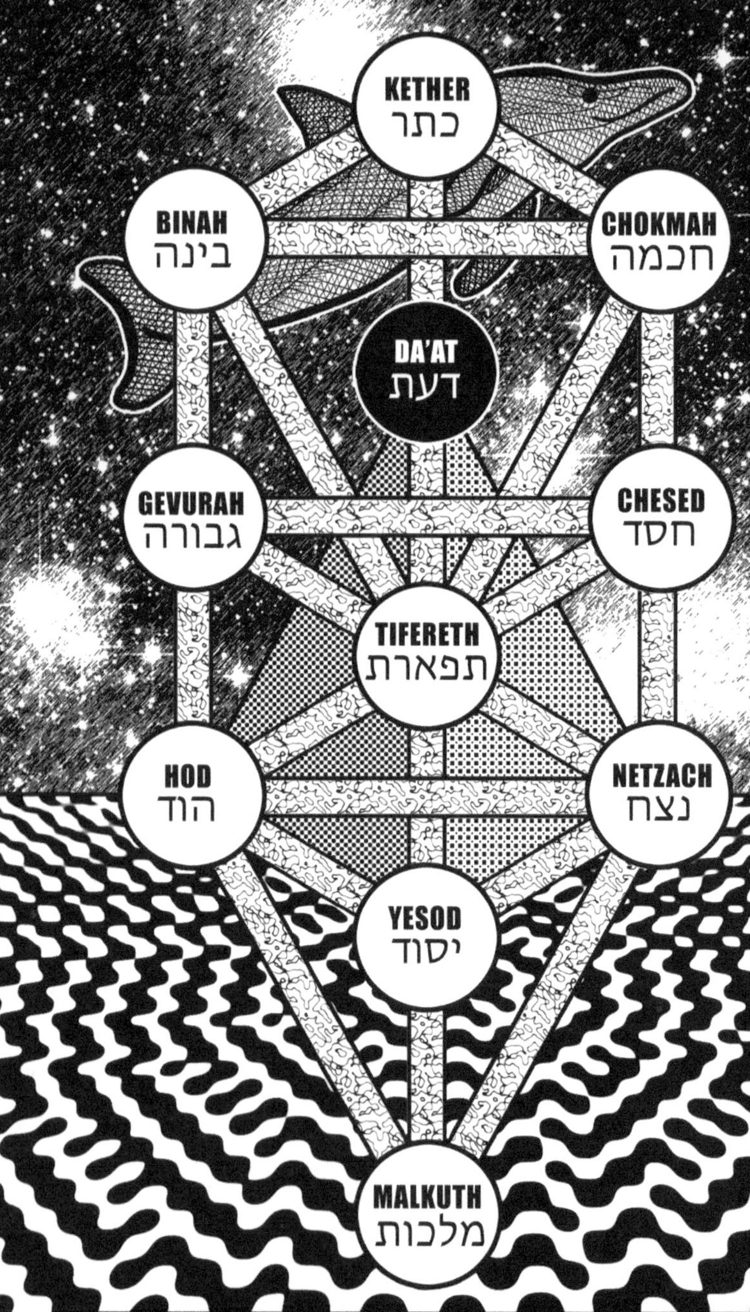

KETHER כתר
BINAH בינה
CHOKMAH חכמה
DA'AT דעת
GEVURAH גבורה
CHESED חסד
TIFERETH תפארת
HOD הוד
NETZACH נצח
YESOD יסוד
MALKUTH מלכות
PREPARE THE CANDIDATE

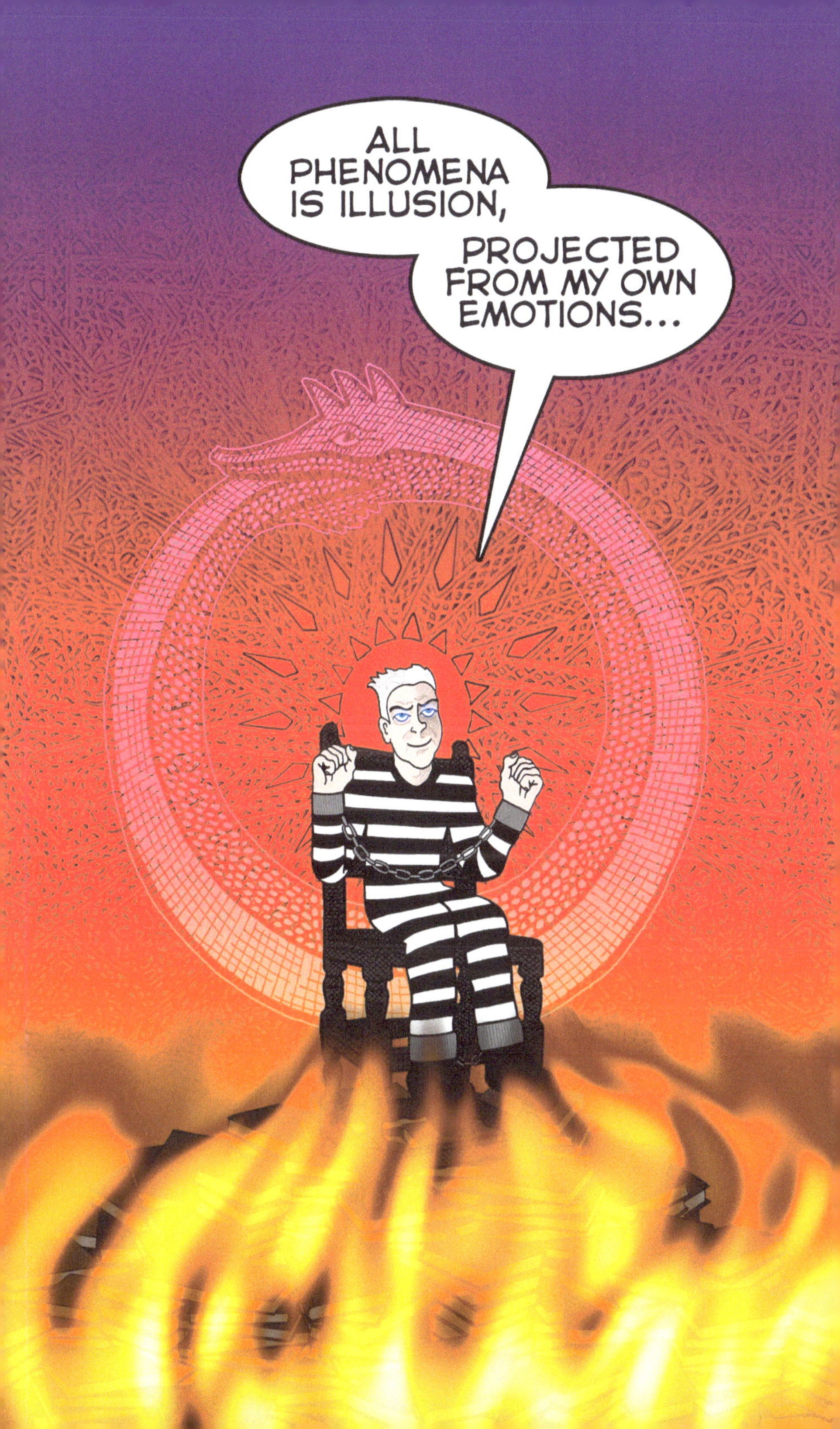

ALL PHENOMENA IS ILLUSION,
PROJECTED FROM MY OWN EMOTIONS...

ALAS, TRAPPED AGAIN IN THE ABYSS OF HALLUCINATIONS.

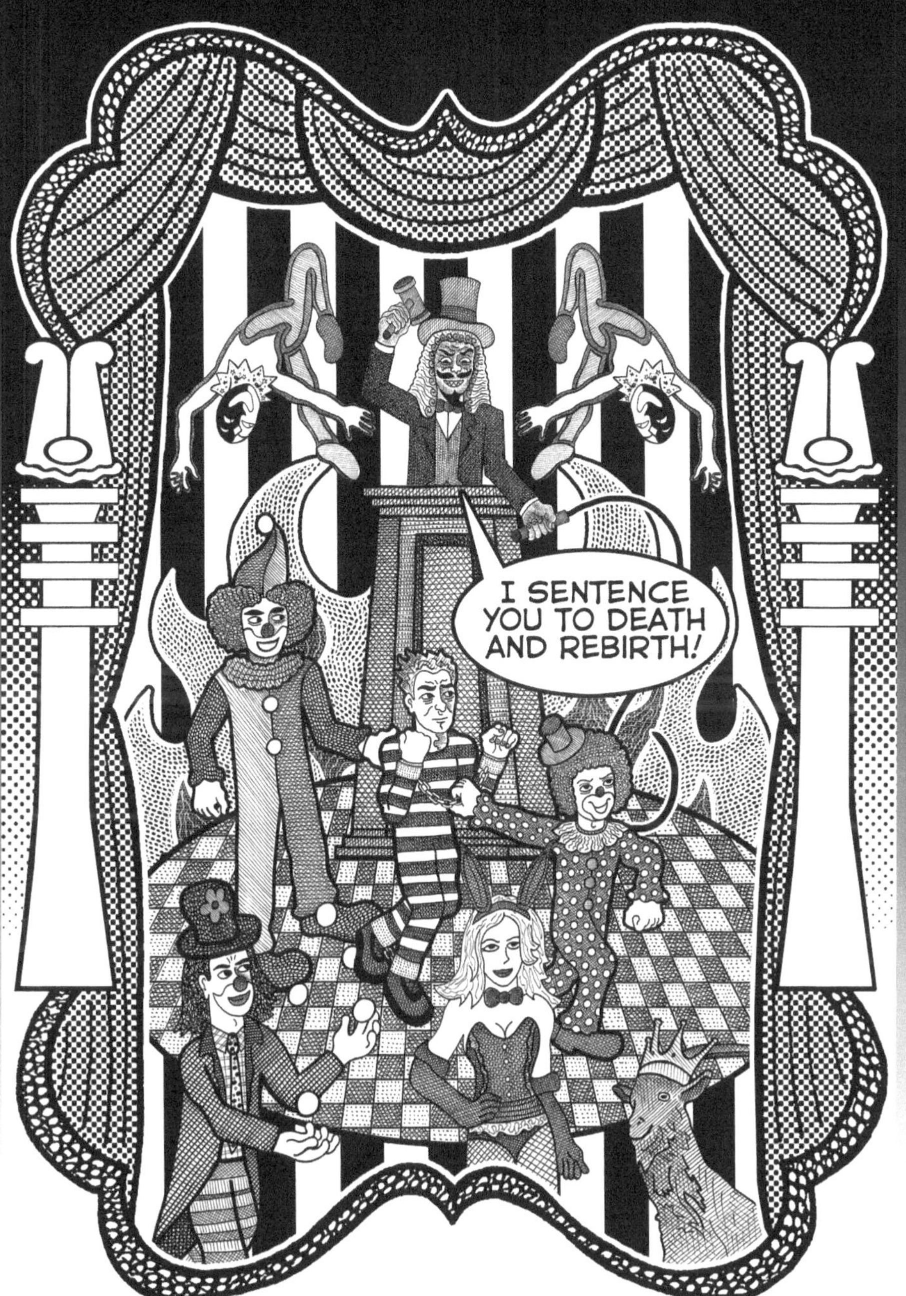

I SENTENCE YOU TO DEATH AND REBIRTH!

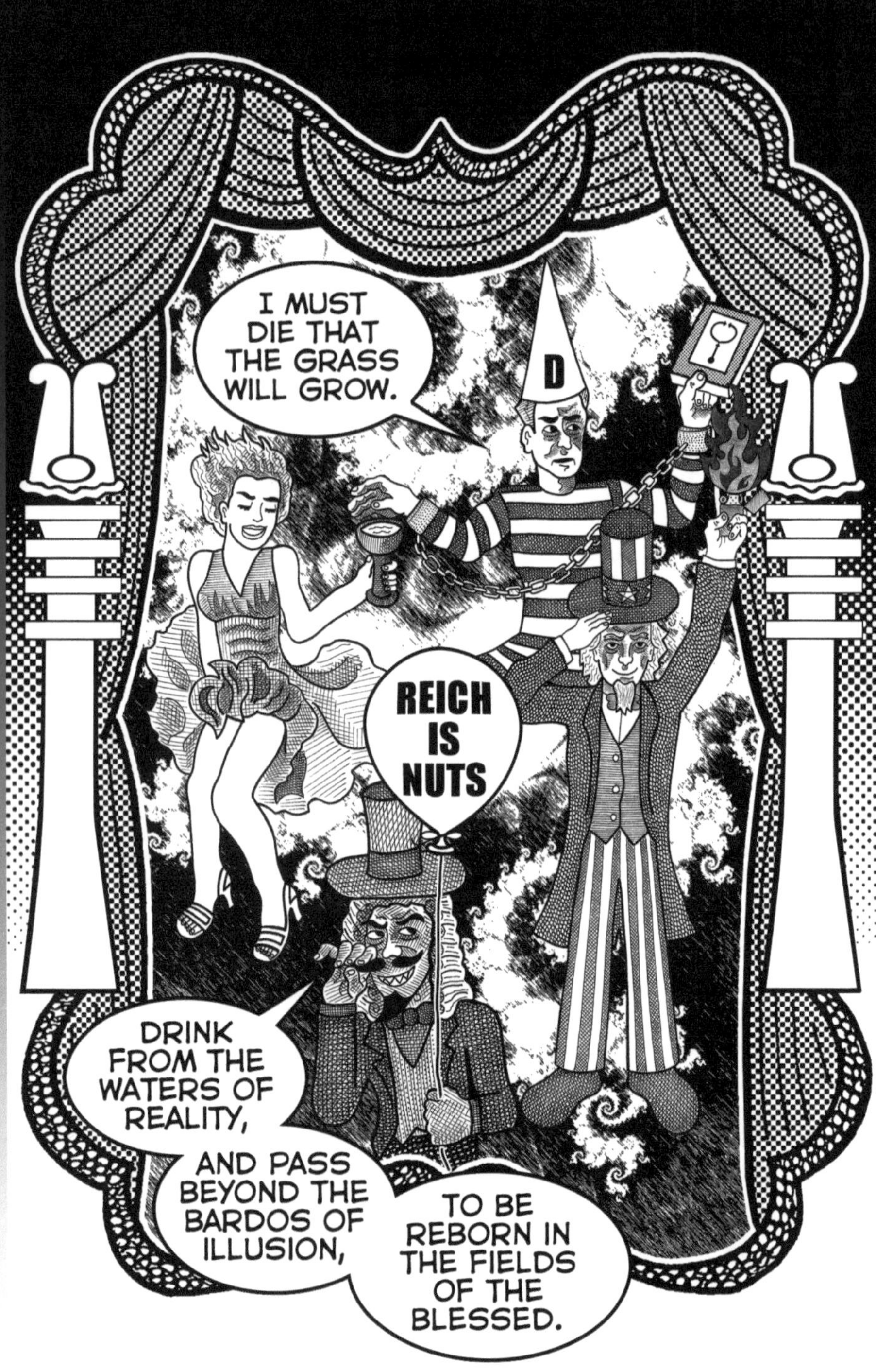

I MUST DIE THAT THE GRASS WILL GROW.
D
REICH IS NUTS
DRINK FROM THE WATERS OF REALITY,
AND PASS BEYOND THE BARDOS OF ILLUSION,
TO BE REBORN IN THE FIELDS OF THE BLESSED.

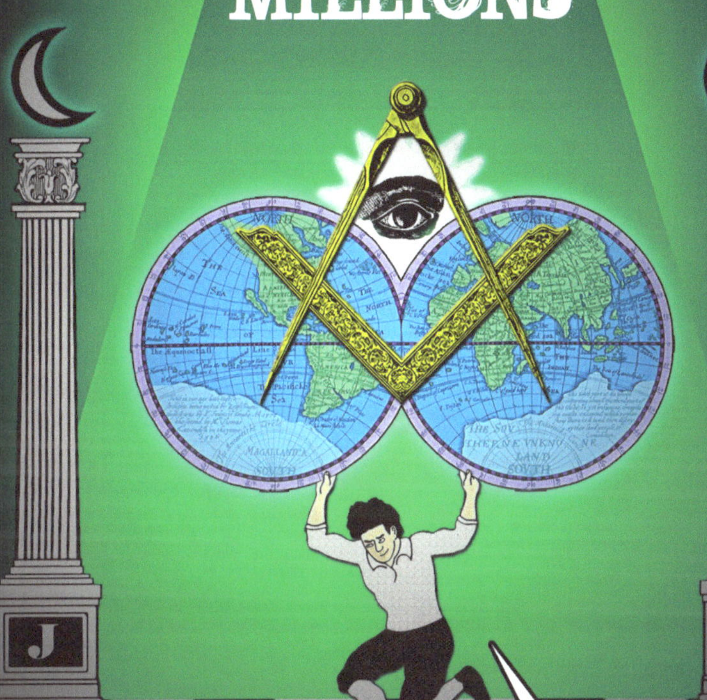

I WILL RETURN AS MILLIONS
J
B
LA TERRA TREMA!
THE EARTH WILL SHAKE!

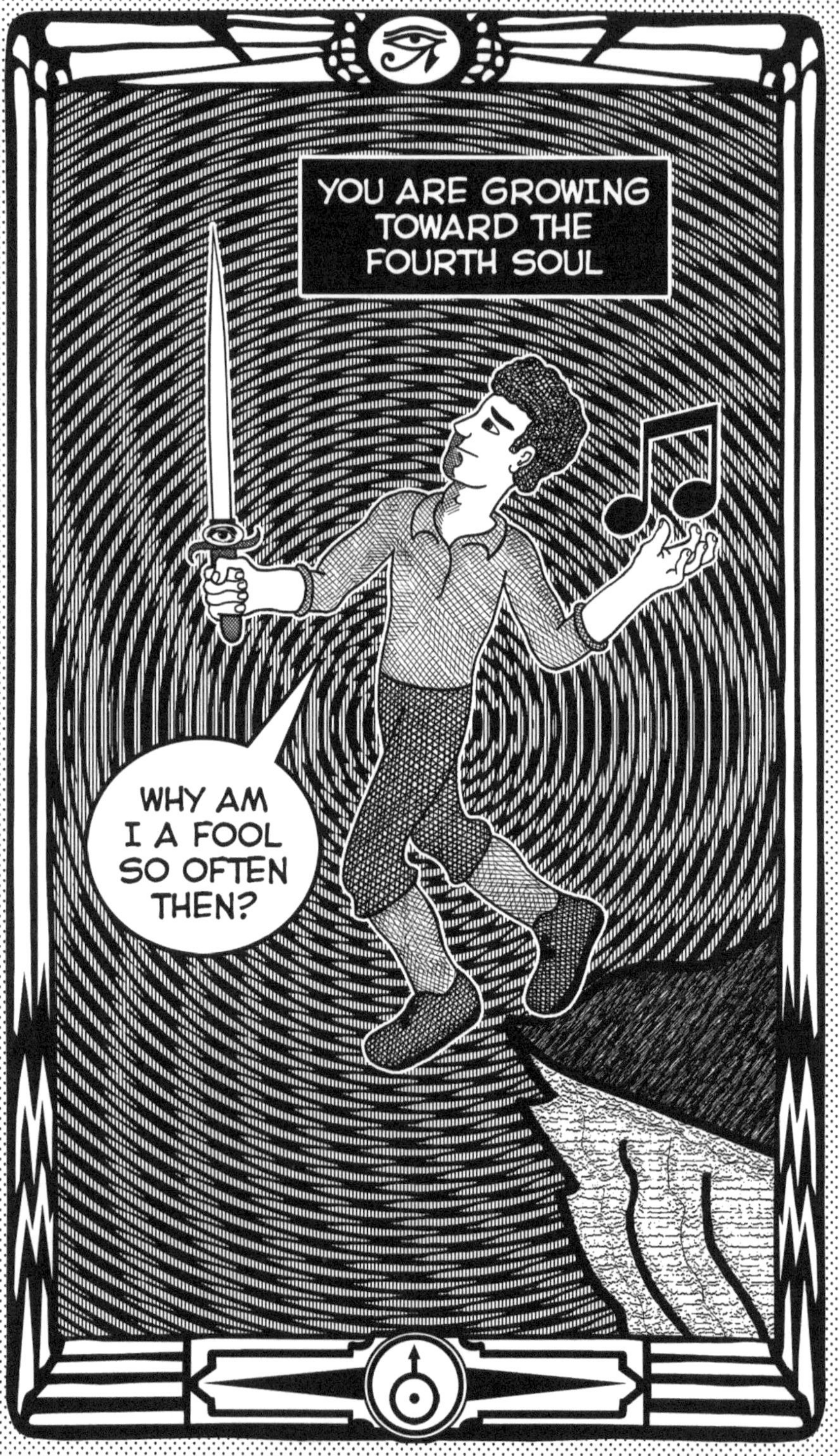

YOU ARE GROWING TOWARD THE FOURTH SOUL
WHY AM I A FOOL SO OFTEN THEN?

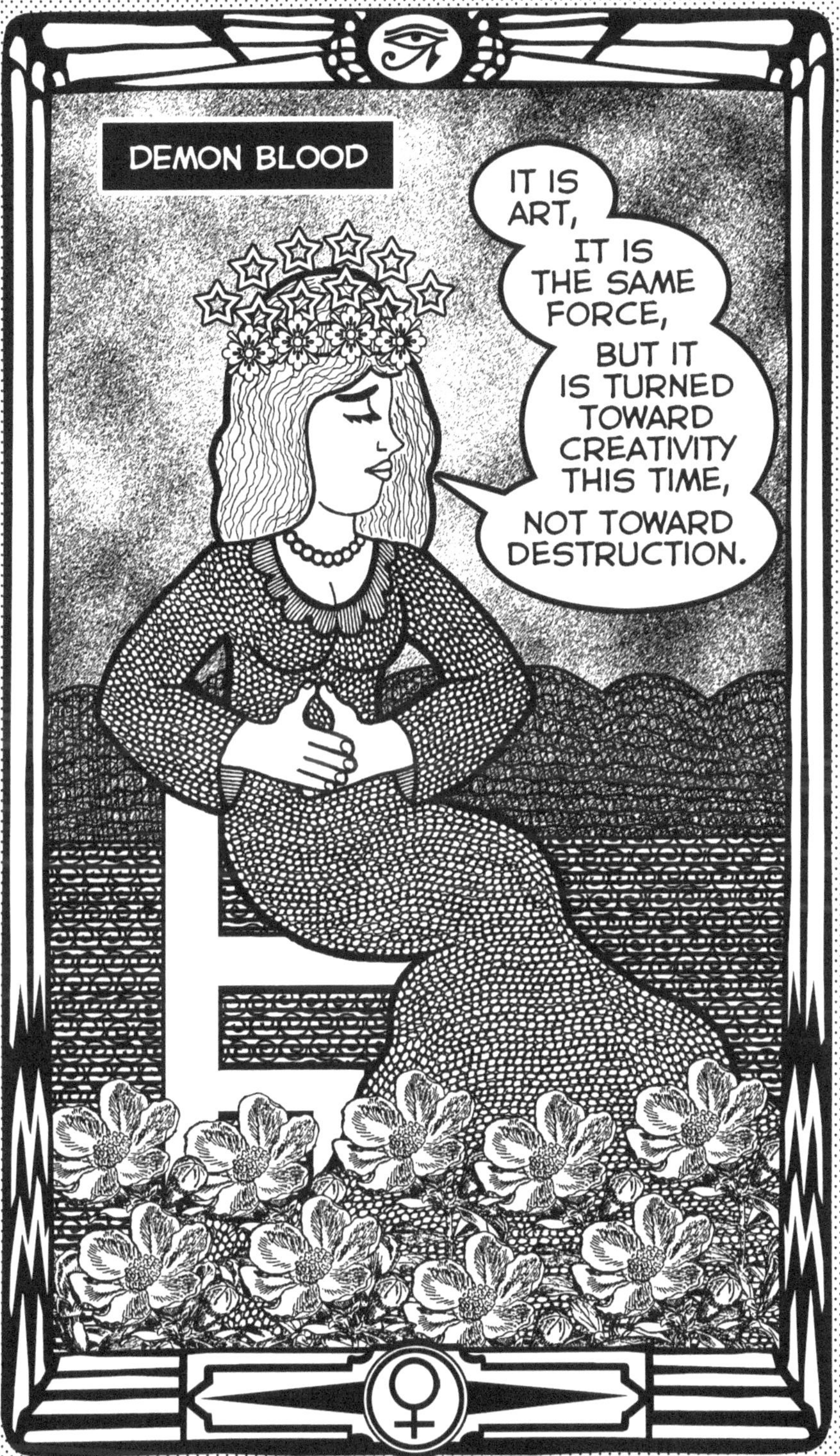

DEMON BLOOD
IT IS ART, IT IS THE SAME FORCE, BUT IT IS TURNED TOWARD CREATIVITY THIS TIME, NOT TOWARD DESTRUCTION.

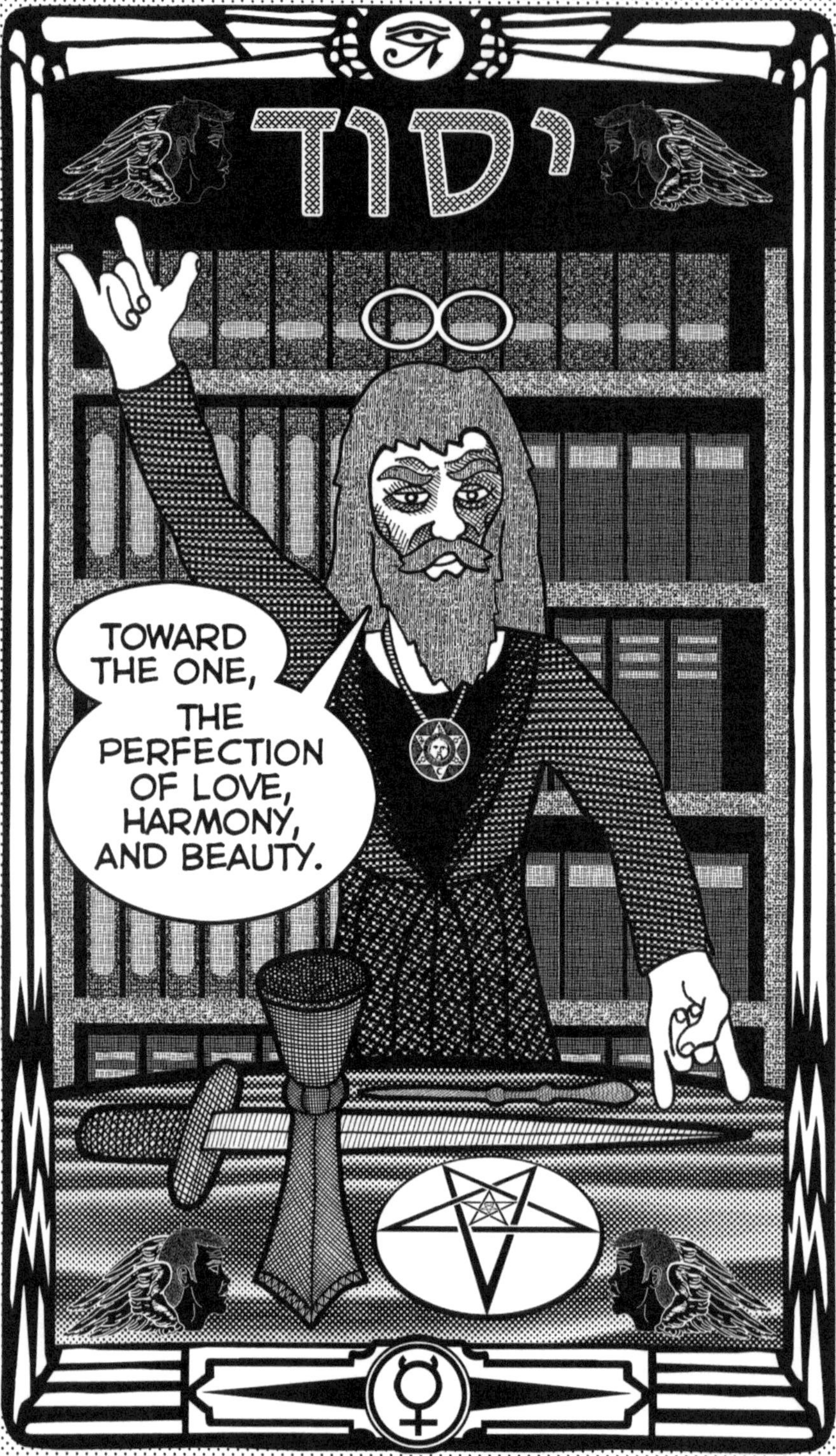

TOWARD THE ONE, THE PERFECTION OF LOVE, HARMONY, AND BEAUTY.

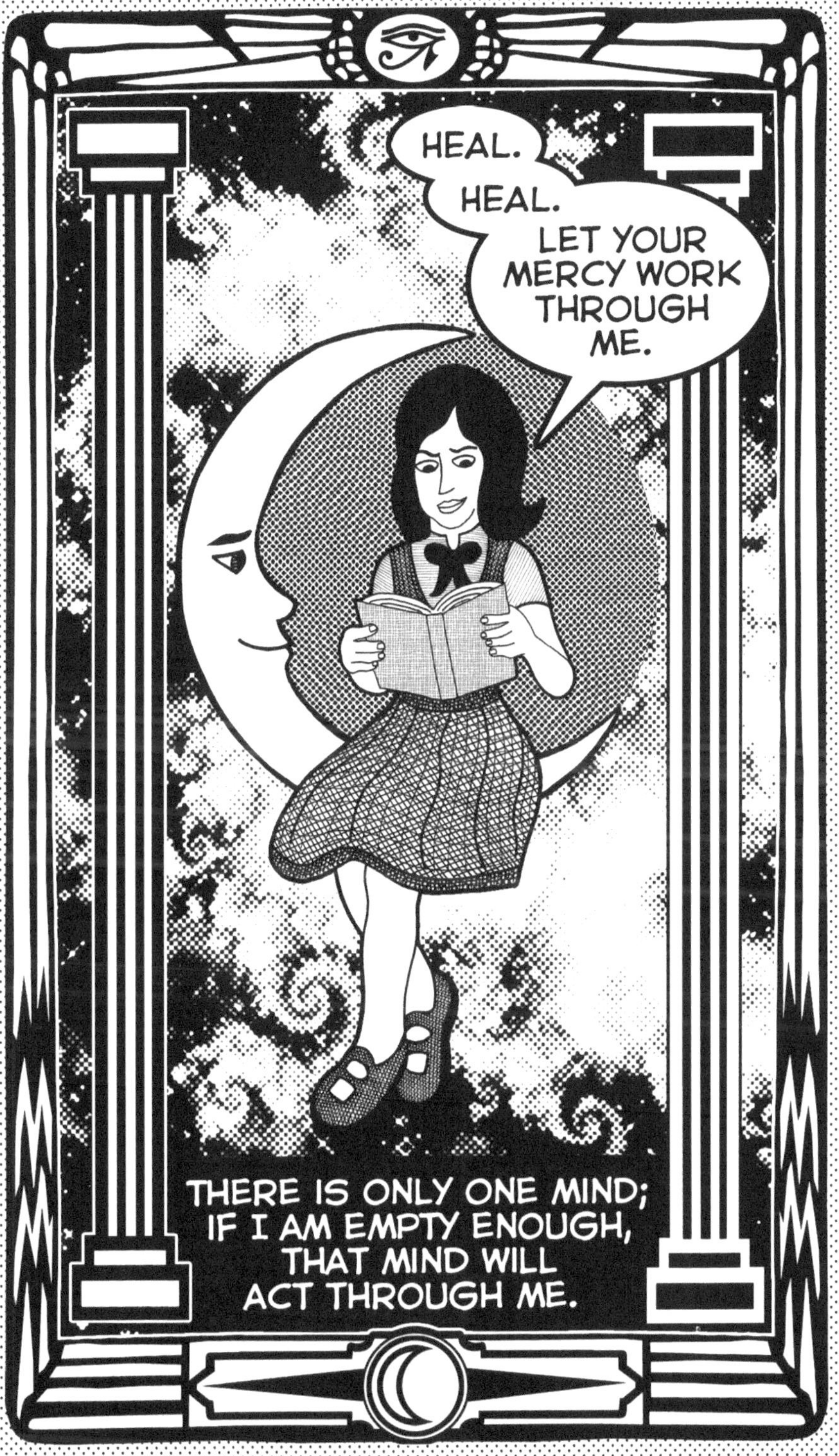

HEAL.
HEAL.
LET YOUR MERCY WORK THROUGH ME.
THERE IS ONLY ONE MIND;
IF I AM EMPTY ENOUGH,
THAT MIND WILL
ACT THROUGH ME.

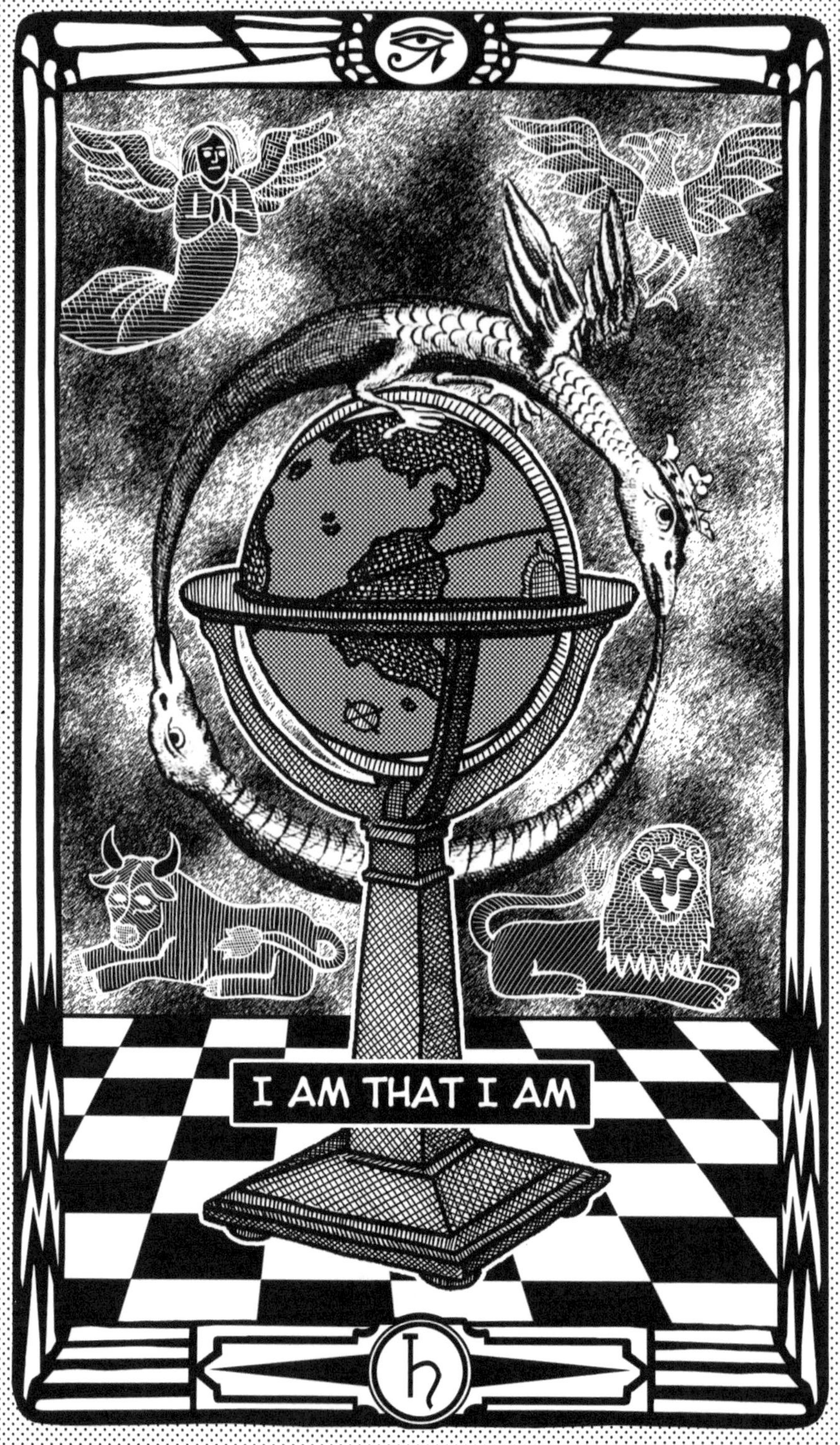

I AM THAT I AM

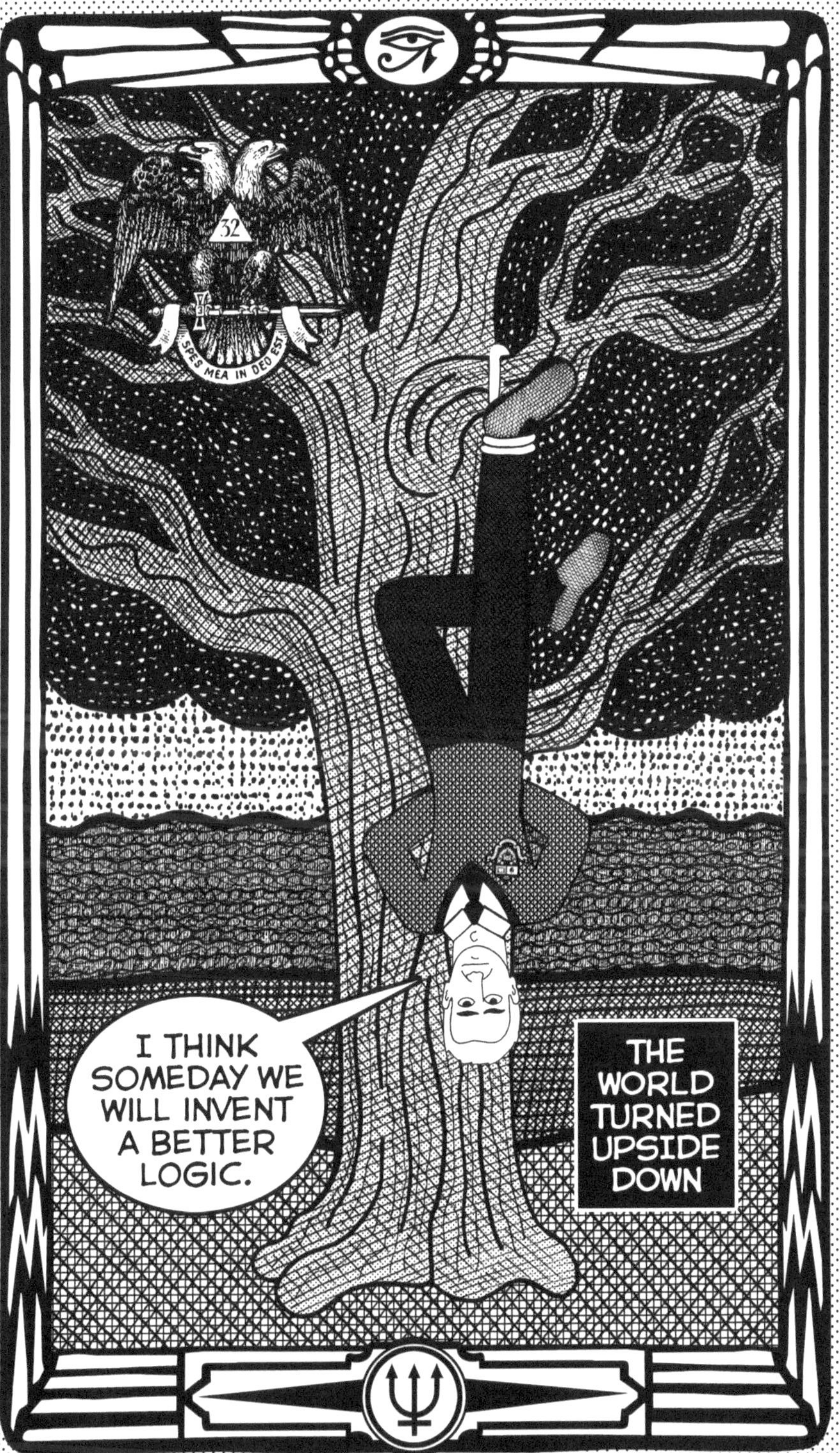
I THINK SOMEDAY WE WILL INVENT A BETTER LOGIC.
THE WORLD TURNED UPSIDE DOWN
SPES MEA IN DEO EST
32

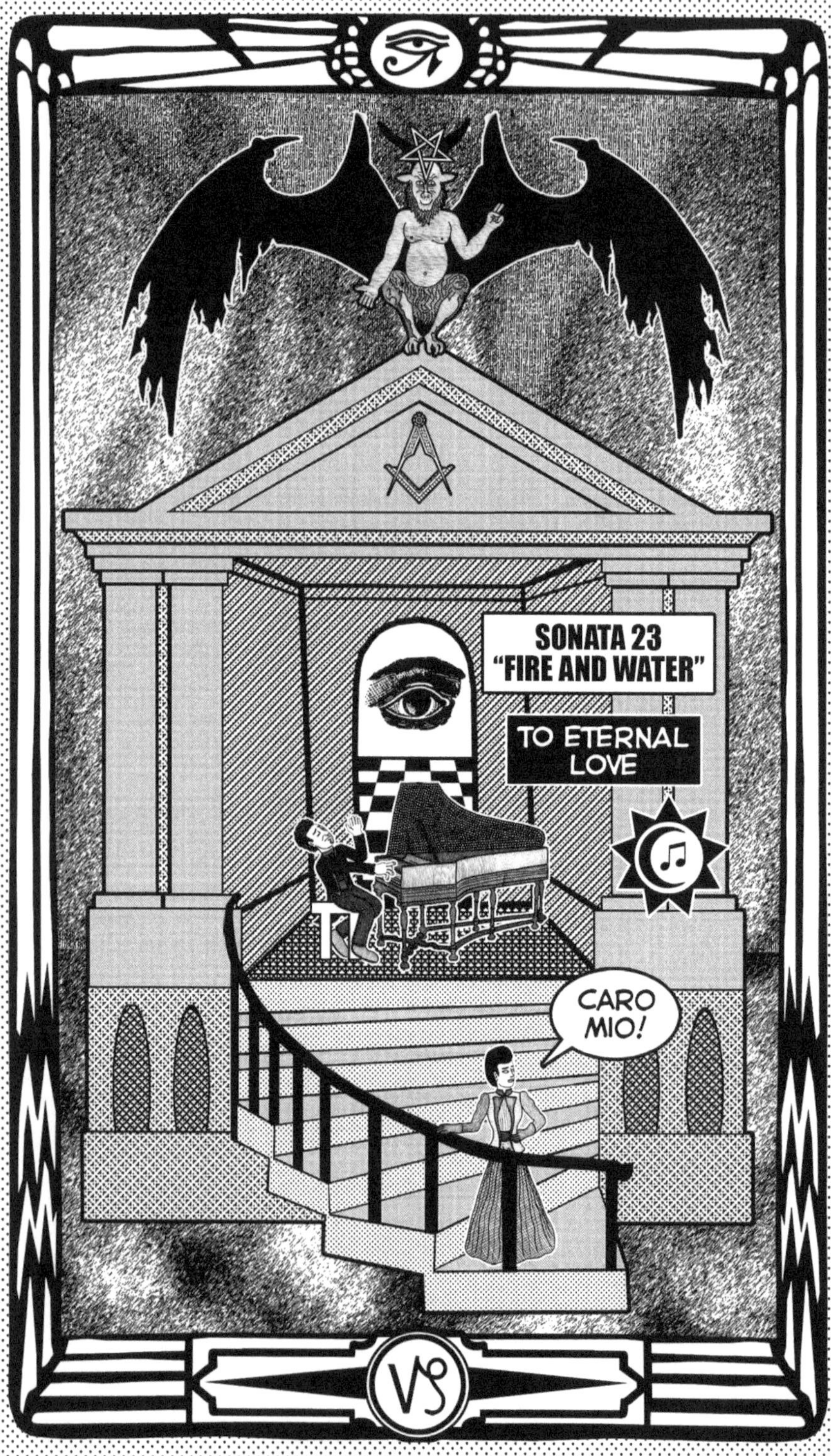

SONATA 23
"FIRE AND WATER"
TO ETERNAL LOVE
CARO MIO!

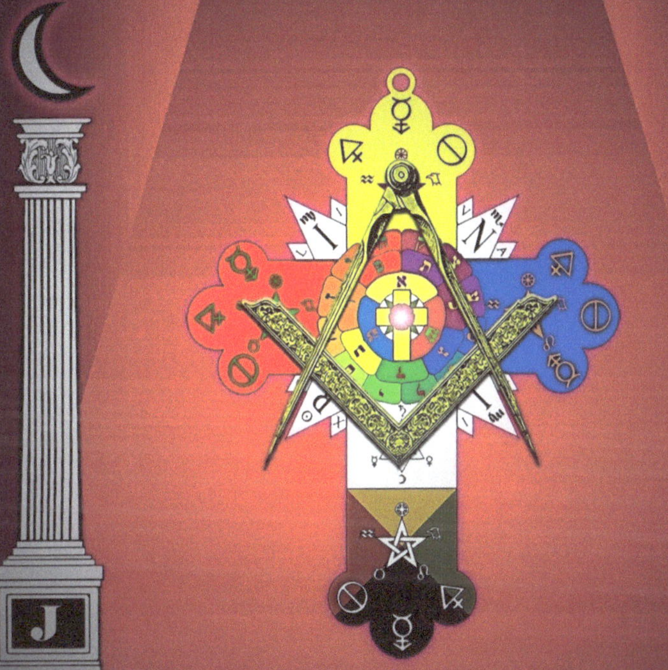

WHO IS NEAR
ME IS NEAR
THE FIRE

THE LOVE THAT MOVES
THE SUN AND OTHER STARS

ET IN ARCADIA EGO

J

B

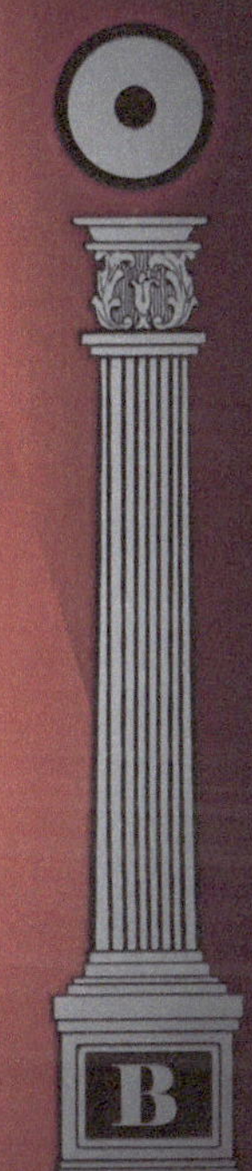

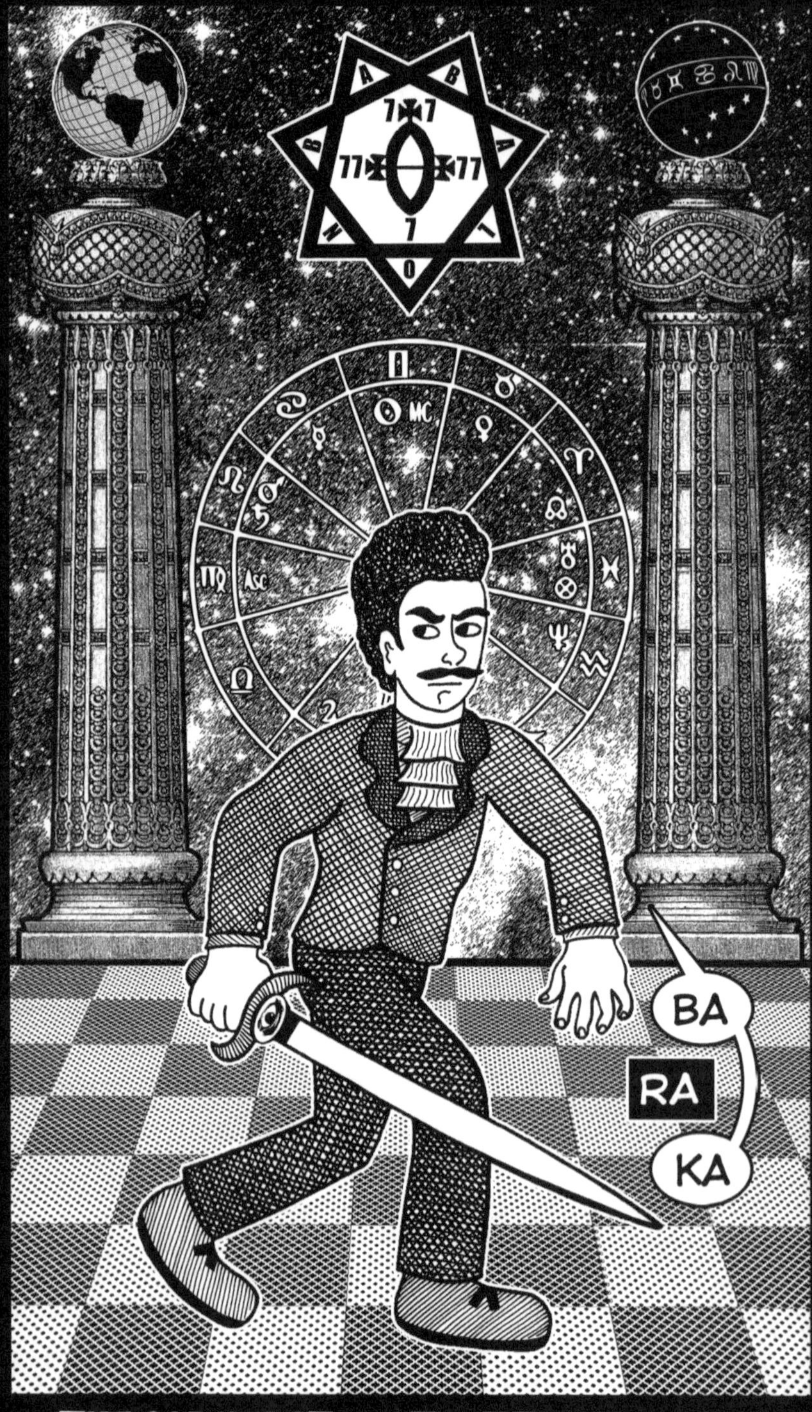

BA
RA
KA
THE CORNERSTONE THAT THE BUILDERS
REJECTED IS THE PLACE FROM WHICH I CAME.

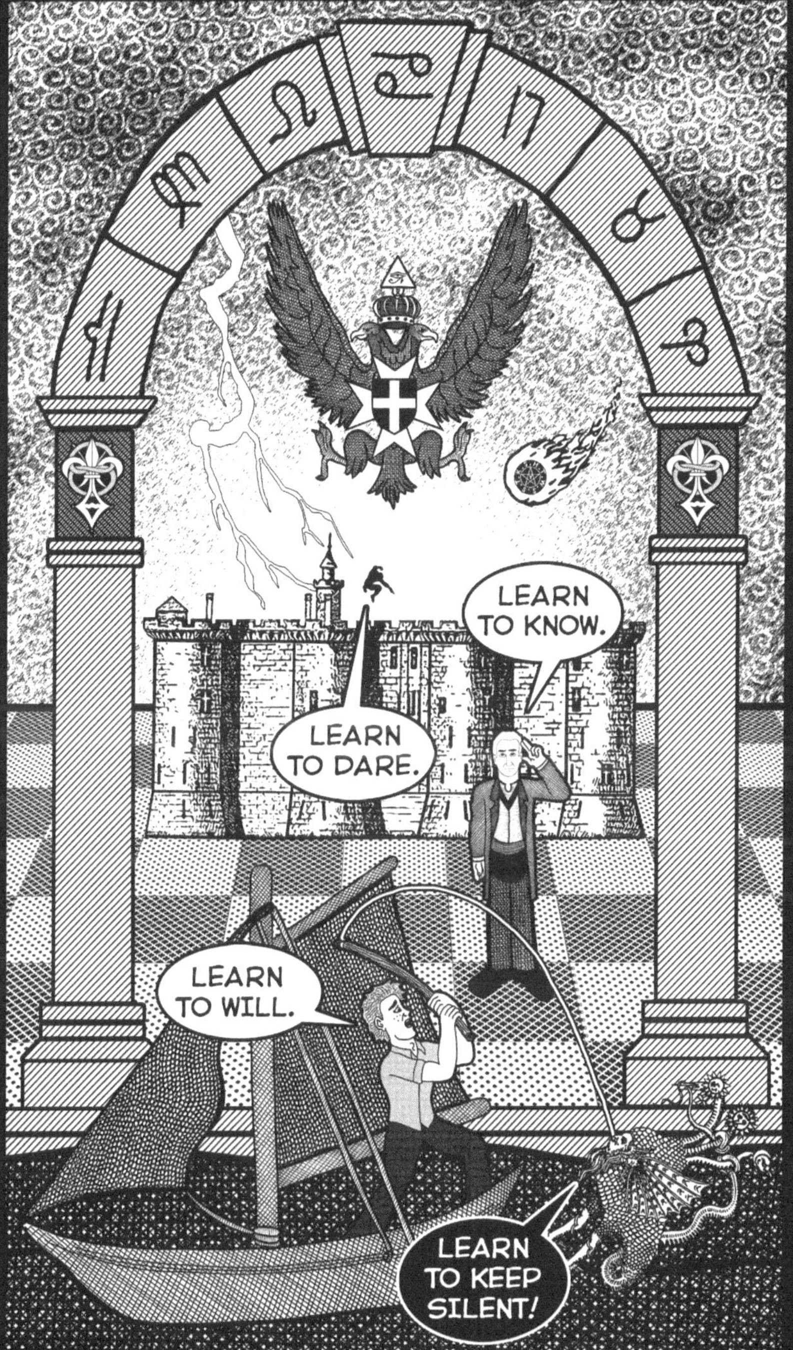

THE GATE THAT IS NOT A GATE IS THE SOURCE OF THE LIVING ONE.

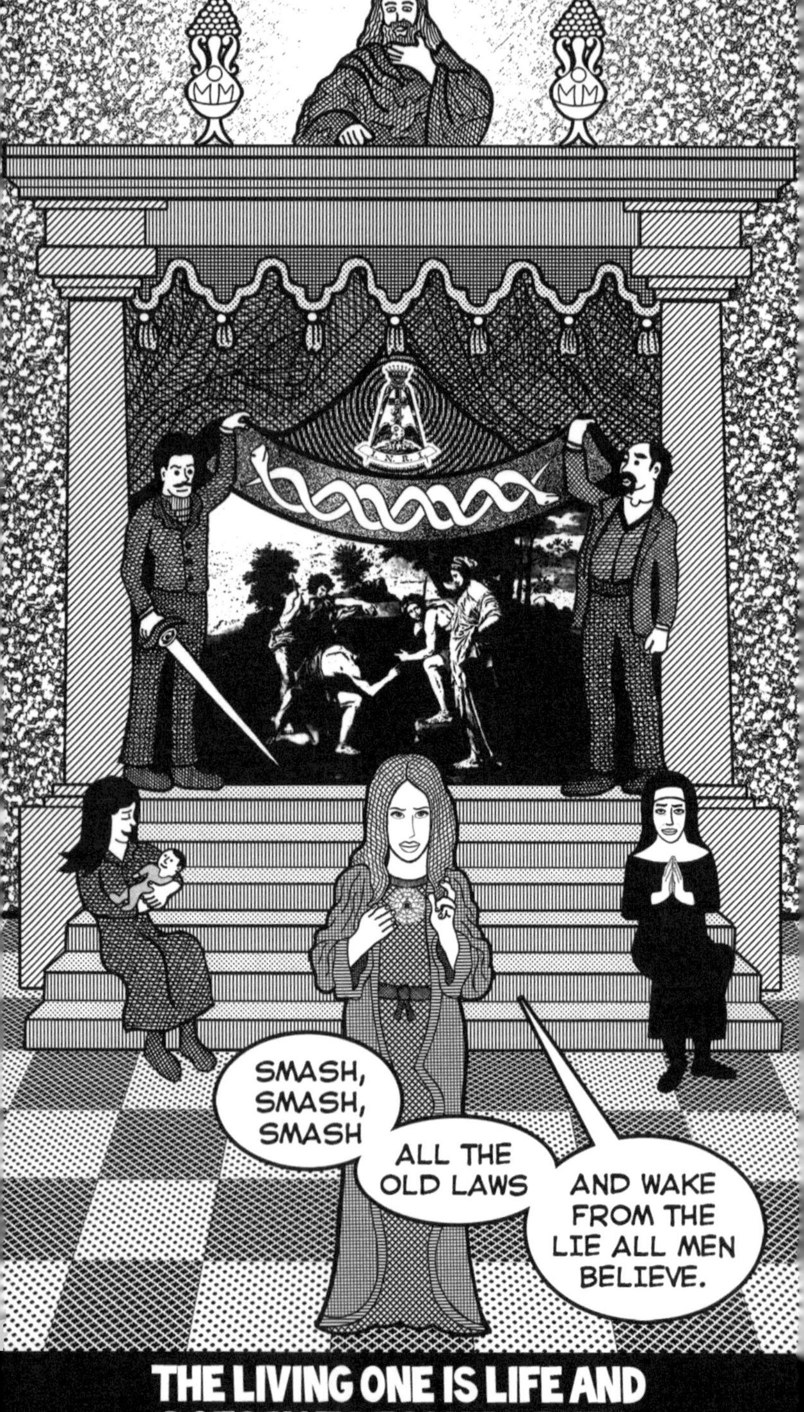

SMASH, SMASH, SMASH
ALL THE OLD LAWS
AND WAKE FROM THE LIE ALL MEN BELIEVE.
THE LIVING ONE IS LIFE AND DOES NOT BECOME DEATH.

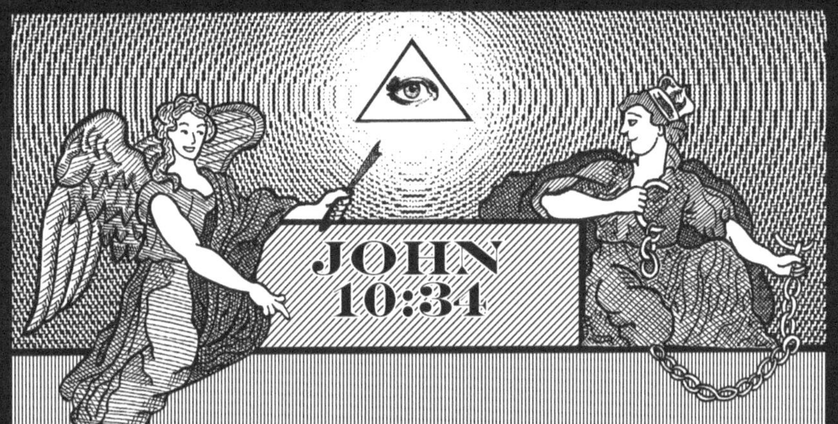

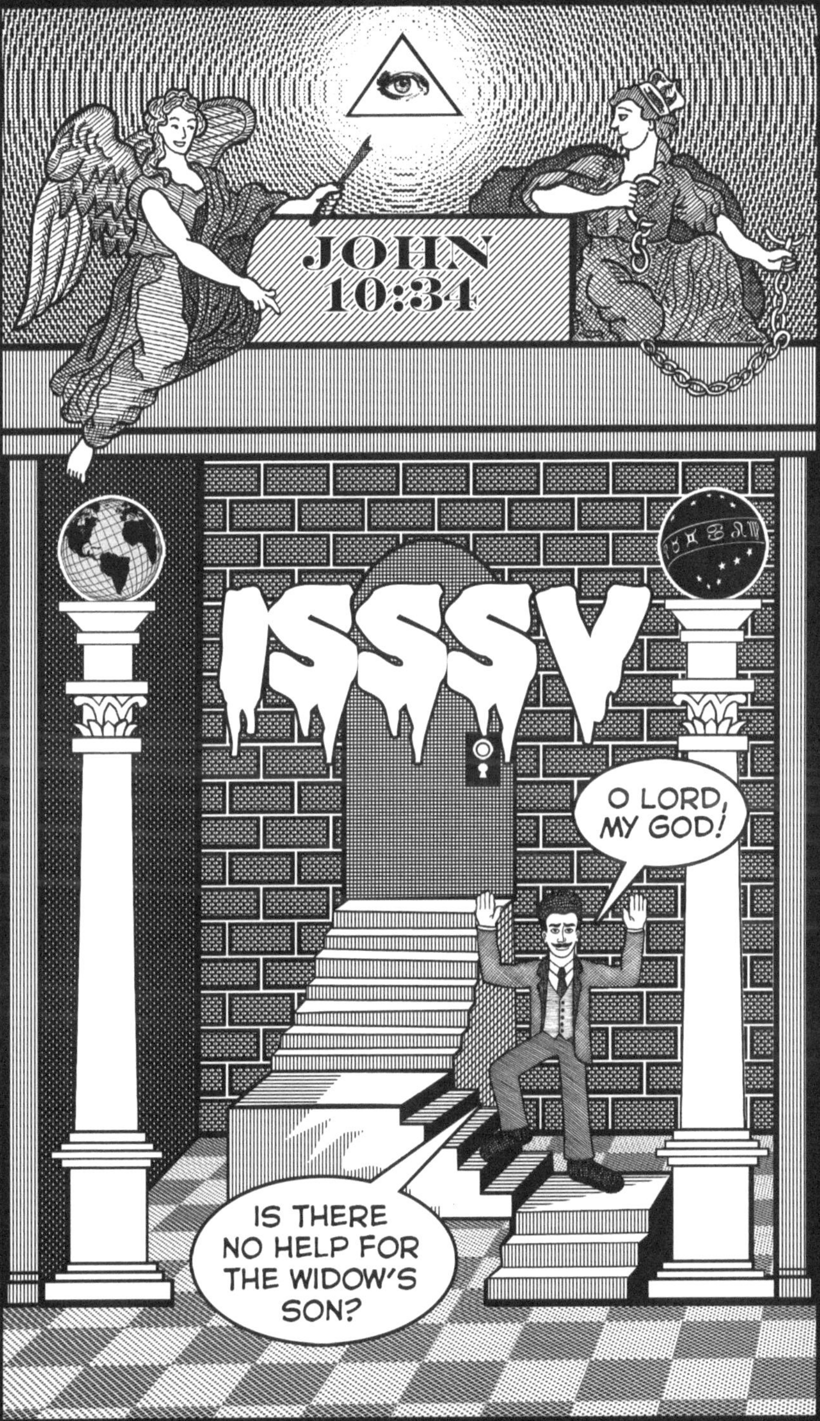

WHO HAS EARS, LET THEM HEAR!

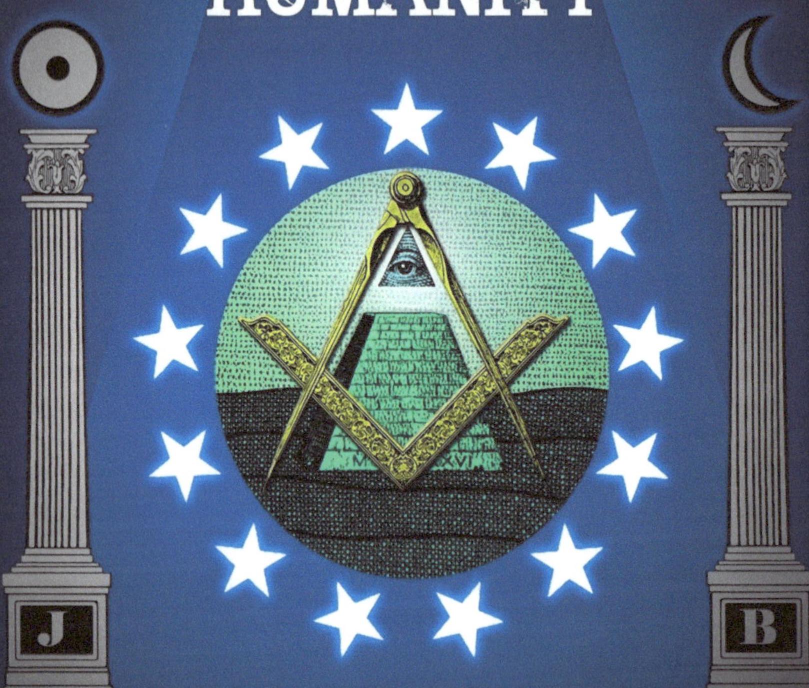

TAKE OFF
THE MASK OF
HUMANITY
J
B
KNOCK. KNOCK. KNOCK.
WHO COMES HERE?
THE SON OF A POOR WIDOW
LADY, SEEKING LIGHT.

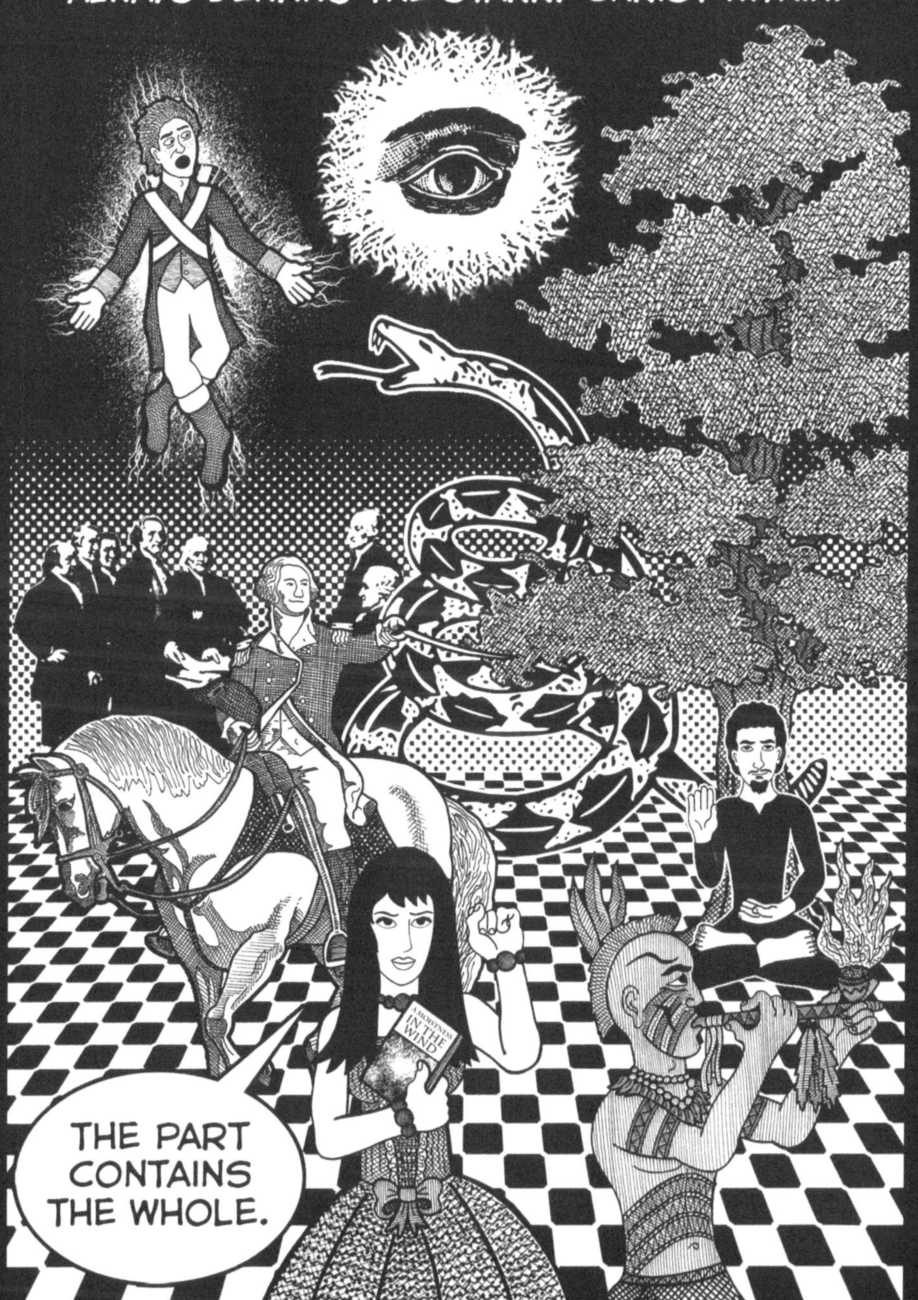

THE TRUE SELF OF EVERY LIVING BEING IS THE ONE GOD. AND YOU GREAT FOOLS, WHO ARE ONLY MASQUES AND SHADOWS OF MEN, ARE ALWAYS DENYING THE STARRY CHRIST WITHIN.
THE PART CONTAINS THE WHOLE.
A MOISTNESS IN THE WIND

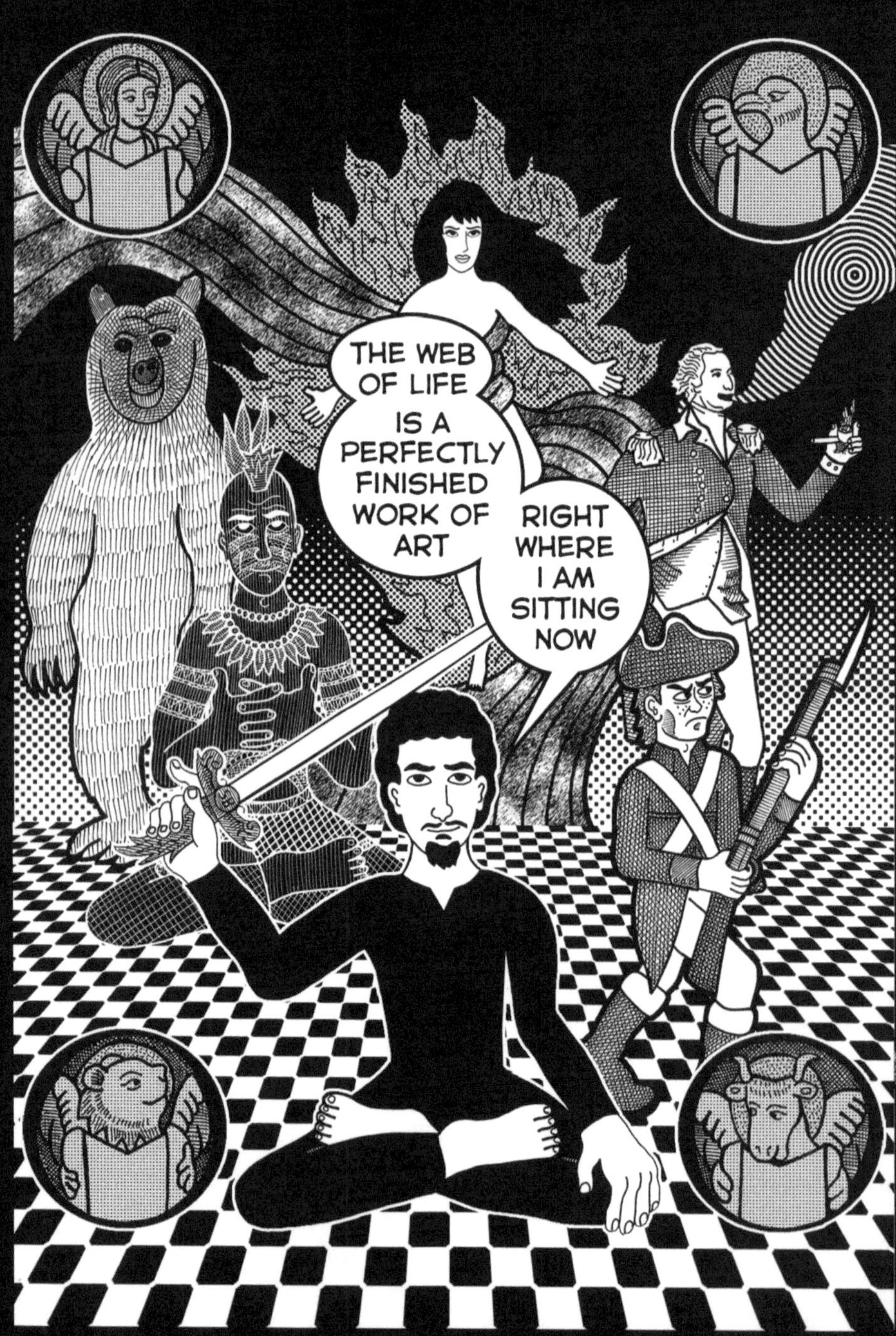

THE WEB OF LIFE
IS A PERFECTLY FINISHED WORK OF ART
RIGHT WHERE I AM SITTING NOW

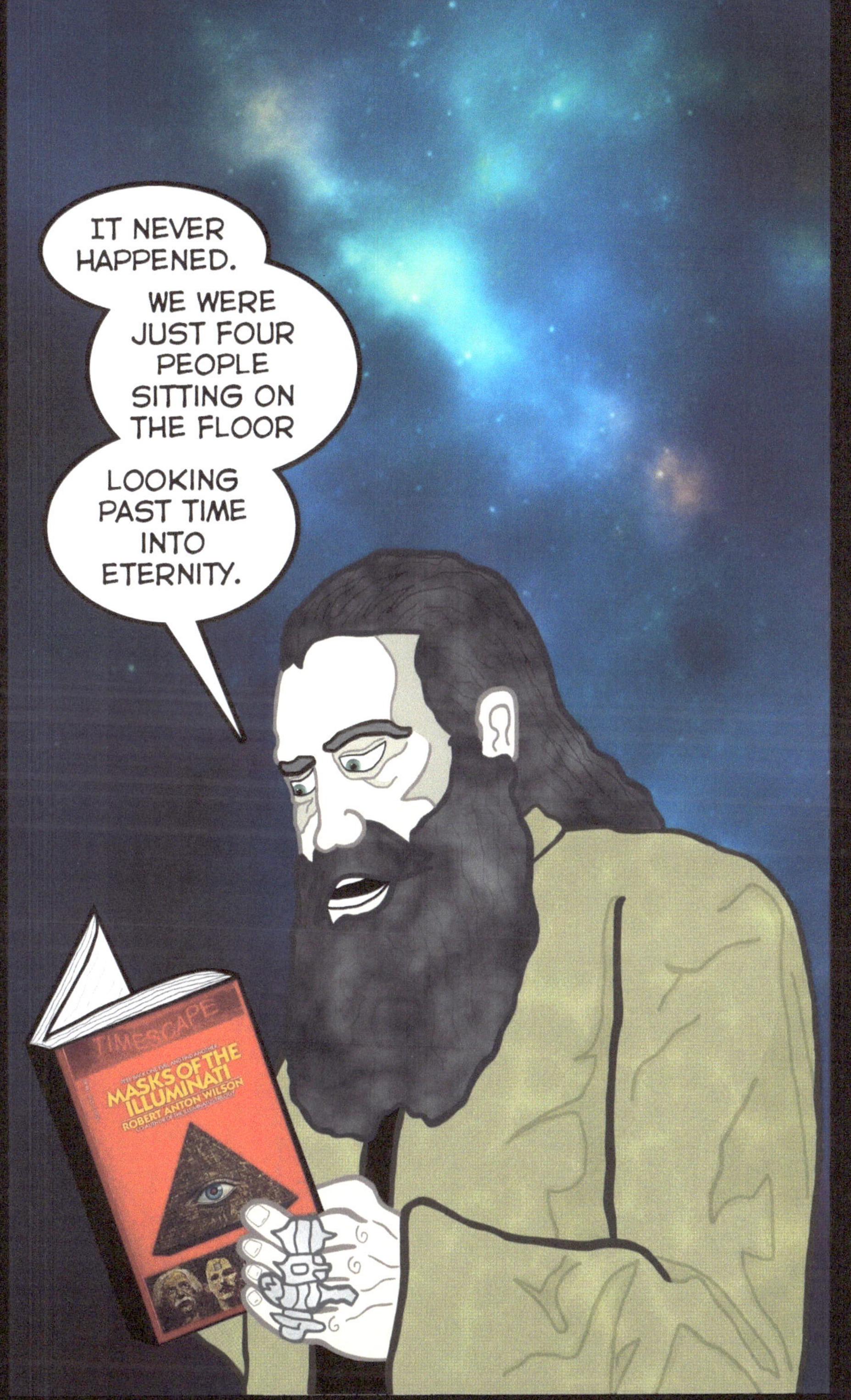

IT NEVER HAPPENED.
WE WERE JUST FOUR PEOPLE SITTING ON THE FLOOR
LOOKING PAST TIME INTO ETERNITY.
TIMESCAPE
MASKS OF THE ILLUMINATI
ROBERT ANTON WILSON

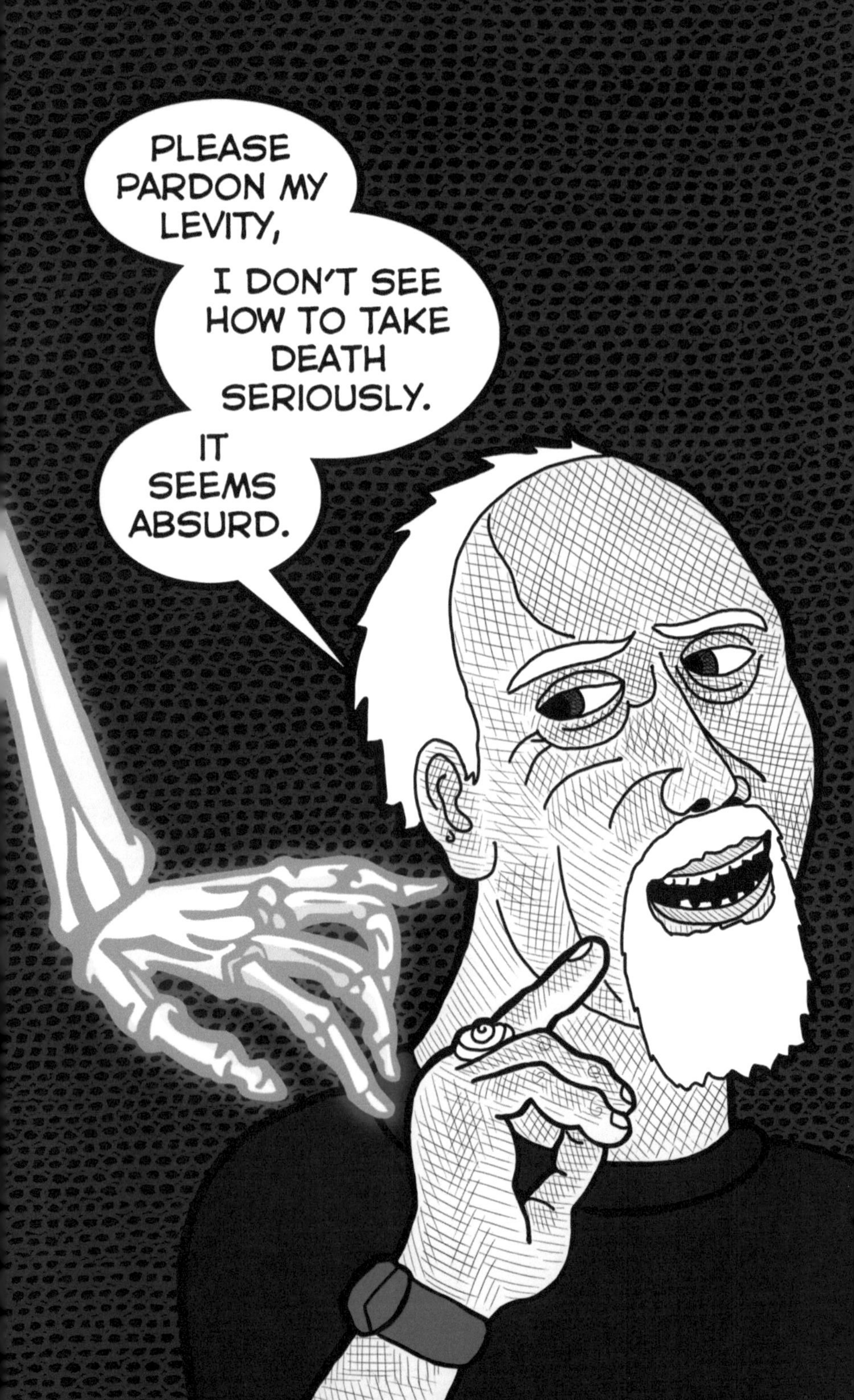

PLEASE PARDON MY LEVITY,
I DON'T SEE HOW TO TAKE DEATH SERIOUSLY.
IT SEEMS ABSURD.

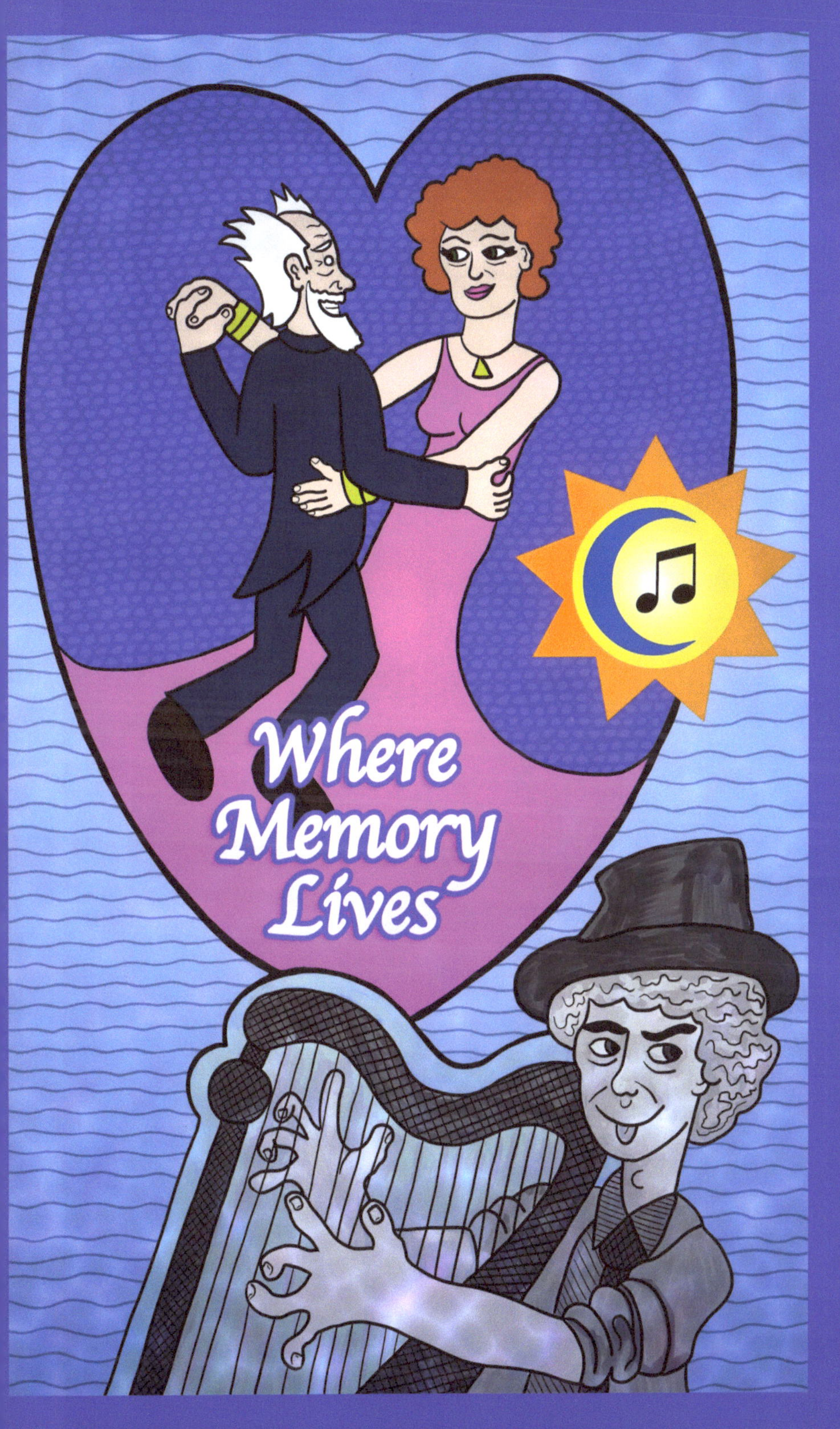
Where
Memory
Lives

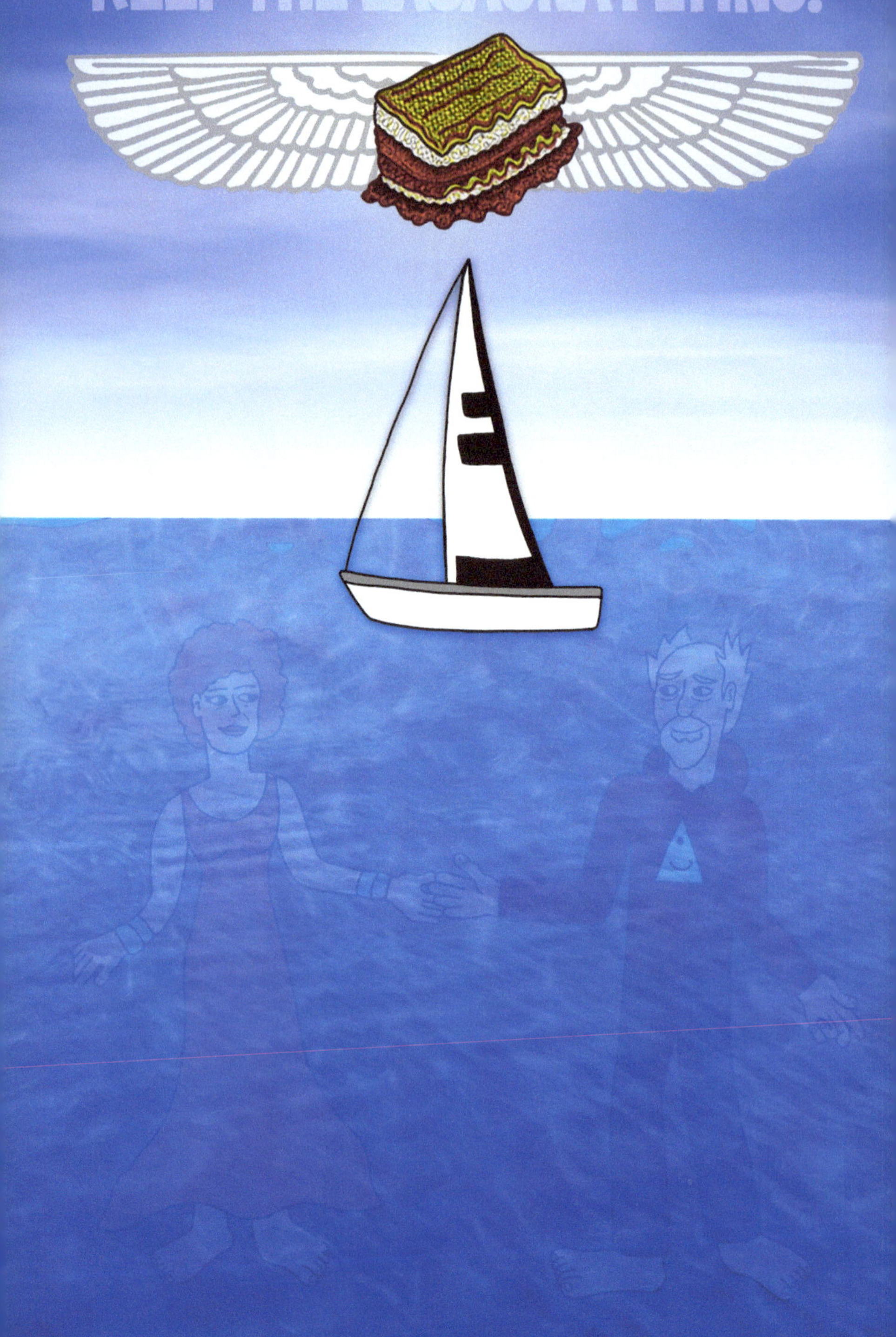

KEEP THE LASAGNA FLYING!

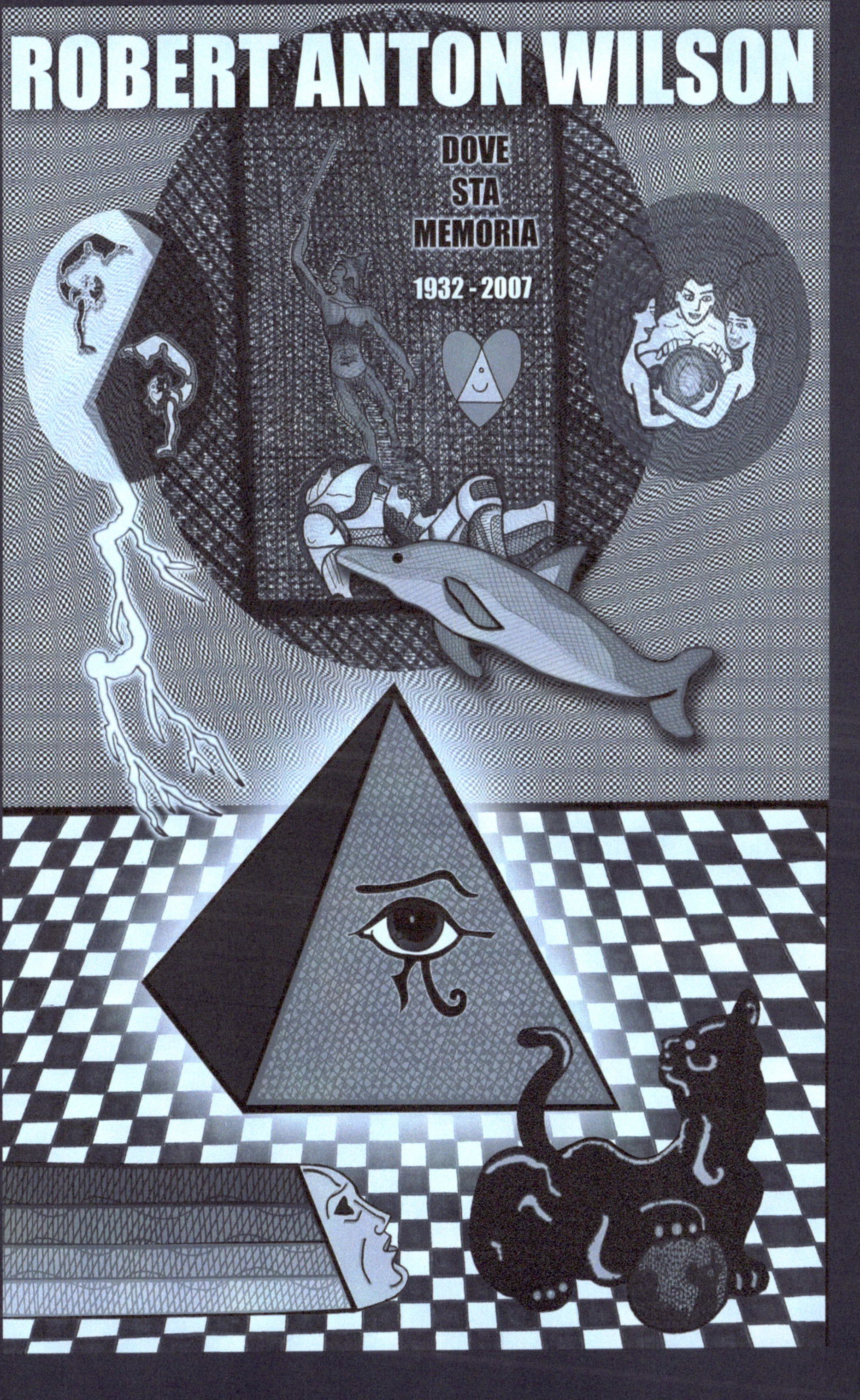

ROBERT ANTON WILSON

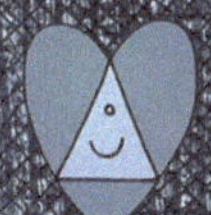

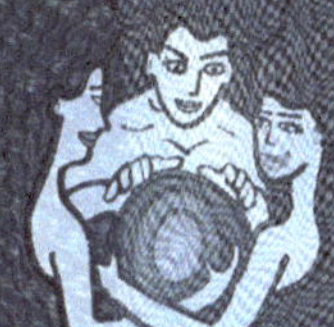

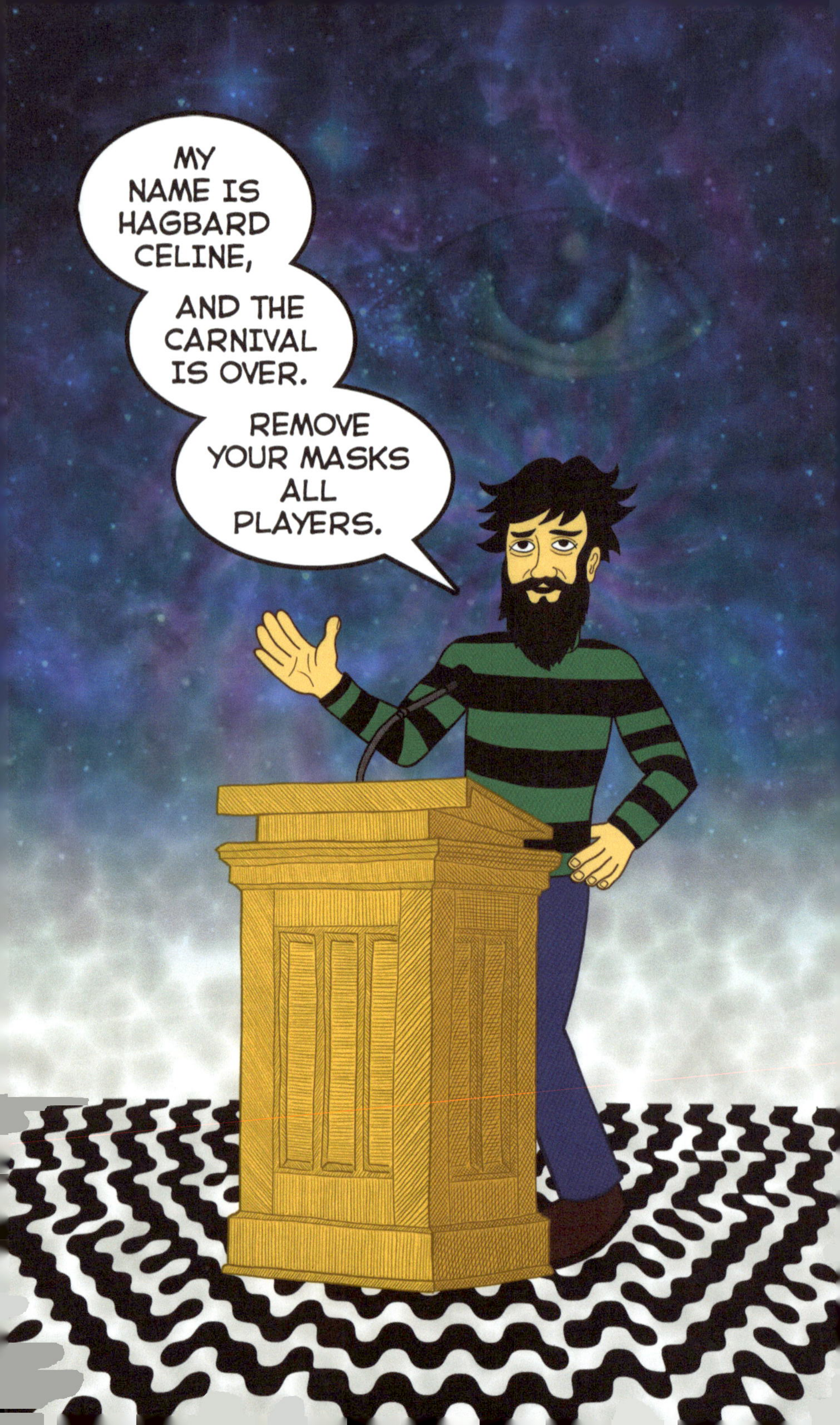

MY NAME IS HAGBARD CELINE,

AND THE CARNIVAL IS OVER.

REMOVE YOUR MASKS ALL PLAYERS.

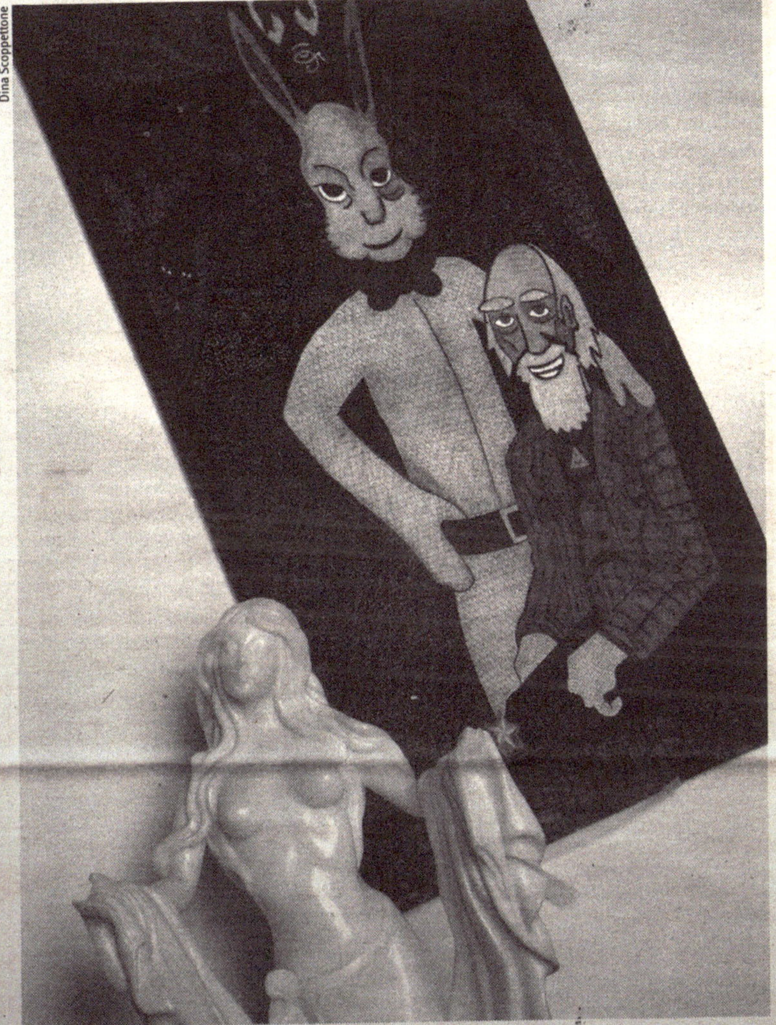

R.A.W. AND HIS POOKAH *'A mischievious creature very fond of rumpots, crackpots and how are you, Mr. Wilson?' says Robert, quoting a line from the film 'Harvey.'*

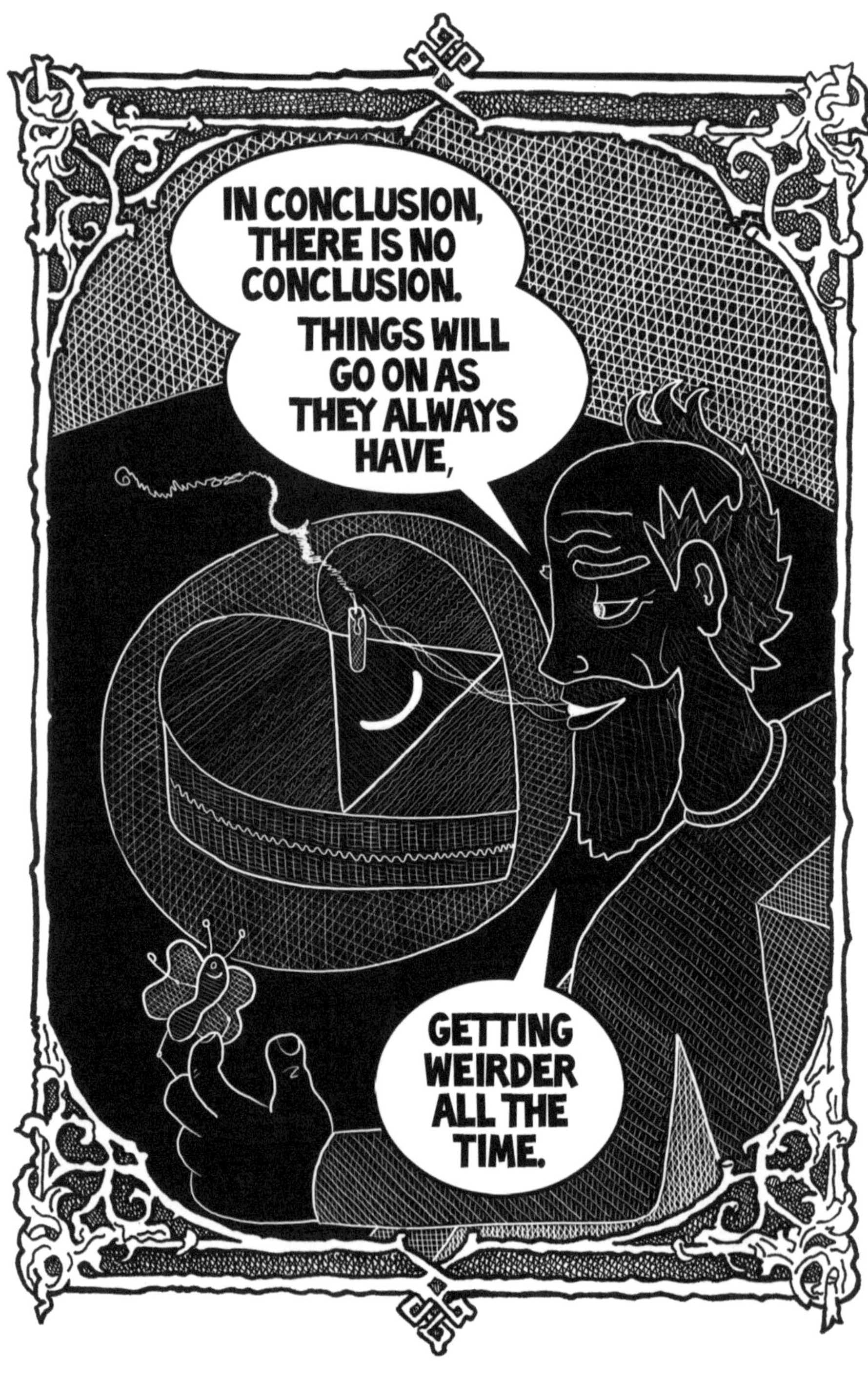

IN CONCLUSION, THERE IS NO CONCLUSION.
THINGS WILL GO ON AS THEY ALWAYS HAVE,
GETTING WEIRDER ALL THE TIME.